SPCM 200

SPEECH COURSEBOOK
10TH EDITION

Karrin Vasby Anderson
Jennifer Emerling Bone
Thomas R. Dunn

Colorado State University

HAYDEN
HM
MᶜNEIL

Hayden-McNeil Sustainability

Hayden-McNeil's standard paper stock uses a minimum of 30% post-consumer waste. We offer higher % options by request, including a 100% recycled stock. Additionally, Hayden-McNeil Custom Digital provides authors with the opportunity to convert print products to a digital format. Hayden-McNeil is part of a larger sustainability initiative through Macmillan Higher Ed. Visit http://sustainability.macmillan.com to learn more.

Printed in the United States of America

10 9 8 7 6 5 4 3 2 1

ISBN 978-0-7380-7156-5

Hayden-McNeil Publishing
14903 Pilot Drive
Plymouth, MI 48170
www.hmpublishing.com

Dunn 7156-5 F14

TABLE OF CONTENTS

SPCM 200 SPEECH COURSEBOOK

SPCM 200: Public Speaking

Contact Hours: 3-0-0 | Mode of Instruction: Face-to-Face

Department of Communication Studies | Colorado State University

Instructor (multiple): _____ Office Hours: _____

COURSE DESCRIPTION

Description from CSU Catalog:
Fundamentals of public speaking, emphasizing content, organization, delivery, and audience response.

Intended Learning Outcomes:
By the end of this course, students who successfully complete SPCM 200 will:

- Become more competent speakers in public settings

- Learn about and perform different genres of public speaking (informative, invitational, persuasive, and commemorative)

- Understand communication theories applicable to public speaking

- Enhance their critical thinking and listening skills

Required Texts:
All students enrolled in SPCM 200: Public Speaking are required to purchase both the class textbook (Griffin's *Invitation to Public Speaking,* 5th edition) and the department's *SPCM 200: Speech Coursebook.* NOTE: Students enrolled in a Service Learning section of SPCM 200 should purchase the Service Learning Edition of the *SPCM 200: Speech Coursebook.* Additional readings, videos, and resources may be posted for free on the class's RamCT site.

COURSE POLICIES

Attendance:
The credits you earn in this class are based on participation as well as performance. The learning experience is not confined to exams you take and speeches you give. A public speaking course involves not just speaking, but also listening, critique, feedback, and facilitation. In addition, speakers need an audience on performance days. Consequently, regular attendance and participation is required. Because illnesses and emergencies do arise during the course of the semester, one week's worth of absences are allowed without penalty:

Fall/Spring Semester
50-minute class: 3 unpenalized absences
75-minute class: 2 unpenalized absences

Summer 4-week session: 1 unpenalized absence
Summer 8-week session: 2 unpenalized absences

Provided it is not a performance or exam day, no explanation is required for the missed day; however, the student is responsible for obtaining any lecture material, handouts, or announcements covered in class. These absences should be reserved for illness, emergencies, family engagements,

x

and participation in university-sponsored activities. **After your unpenalized absences have been used, each unexcused absence will result in a 15 points per absence deduction from your final grade (30 points during the 4-week Summer sessions).** If your social, academic, extracurricular, or employment schedule will interfere with attendance and participation in SPCM 200, *please consider taking this course a different semester.*

Attendance on Speech Days: You must attend class on days you are scheduled to give a speech. **Failure to give your speech on the assigned day will result in the grade of "zero" for that assignment.**

Excused Absences: Occasionally, a student may miss a speech or have an extra absence for which they may not be penalized. There are five standards by which we determine if an absence is excused. Before asking your instructor for an exemption, however, be certain that your situation conforms to *every one* of the following criteria:

1. The absence must be unexpected. There was no way you could prepare for it or plan ahead.

2. The circumstances of your absence must be beyond your control.

3. The nature of your excuse must be serious: a death or medical crisis in your immediate family, onset of an incapacitating illness, or a severe accident.

4. If you are physically able, you must contact your instructor or leave a message prior to the time you are expected to give a speech or complete an assignment.

5. You must be able to document your excuse in writing.

University Activities: If you will miss class due to participation in university-sponsored sports or activities, please discuss your schedule with your instructor *early* in the semester. Provide a letter, signed by a coach or sponsor, verifying your participation in the activity. Absences for events will count as unpenalized absences **(you may not miss 3 classes for activities and then get additional free absences on top of that)**, but if you have more than 3 activity-related absences those can be excused if advance notice and documentation is provided. Please make every effort to schedule your speeches on days that do not conflict with your travel schedule. If your activity requires you to miss more than 4 classes during the course of the semester, please take SPCM 200 a different semester.

Tardiness: Tardiness is particularly disruptive in a public speaking class. **Never** walk in on another student who is giving a speech. Wait at the door until their speech is concluded. Additionally, it is important to come to class on time so that your instructor can make an accurate record of your attendance. If you come to class late, after attendance has been taken, you are *personally responsible* for informing the instructor that you were present. Habitual tardiness may result in the loss of attendance points.

Common Final: During the fall and spring semesters, all SPCM 200 students take a common final exam written by the Director of the Basic Course. All students are required to take the final exam at the time designated in the official university final exam schedule. Students will not be permitted to take the exam early due to travel or other plans, and they will not be able to make it up if they miss it. If students have multiple exams scheduled on the day of the SPCM 200 final and are hoping to rearrange their testing schedule, they should **plan to rearrange their other exams**. Since there are only a few common finals scheduled by the university, they must take precedence.

Cell Phones: Cell phones are also particularly disruptive in a public speaking class. Please turn your phone off prior to entering class. If your cell phone is a continual disruption, your instructor will assess an appropriate penalty.

Topic Selection and Campus Safety: Students will approve all speech topics with their instructor. Though acceptable speech topics will be determined by each individual instructor in conjunction with the expectations of the particular speech assignment, campus safety is a determining factor for all topics in all sections. Therefore, students will not bring any dangerous or illegal objects/substances to their public speaking class, even if intended to enhance a public speaking situation. If a student has questions regarding whether their topic and/or speaking aid is appropriate, they should speak with their instructor at least 48 hours prior to the day they are scheduled to speak.

Signing Up for a Speaking Slot: It is the student's responsibility to sign up for a day to speak for each speech assignment in class. Students who are absent on sign-up days are responsible for contacting the instructor as soon as possible to sign up for a slot. In the event a student is absent on speech sign-up day, it is *possible and likely* that they will automatically be slotted to speak on the first day of speeches. In that event, please plan accordingly.

Computer/Technology Problems:
Computer malfunctions do not constitute an "excuse" or an "emergency." Prepare your assignments far enough in advance so that when your computer malfunctions (*and it will*) you will be able to rectify the problem and turn in the assignment on time. Allow for printer, disk, server, service provider, and other technology problems. Also, have a back-up plan in case classroom technology fails during your speech. You will be expected to go on with the presentation, just as you would if you encountered a technology problem on the job.

Academic Integrity:
Students in SPCM 200 are expected to do their own work. Research, visual aids, and outlines for speeches must be products of a student's individual, original work. You may not work with students in your own or other sections of SPCM 200 on the same speech topic, and any information you obtain from outside sources for use in your speech must be cited orally in the speech and credited in the bibliography. Additionally, **providing another SPCM 200 student a copy of your original work will also be reported to the Conflict Resolution and Student Conduct Service office.** Failure to conform to Colorado State University's standards for academic integrity can result in failure of the assignment, failure of the course, and/or reporting of the student's conduct to the university's Conflict Resolution and Student Conduct Service office. For a detailed explanation of CSU's academic integrity guidelines, see the *General Catalog.*

SafeAssign:
The Department of Communication Studies uses SafeAssign software built into RamCT as a tool to deter plagiarism and educate students on how to properly cite other sources in their work. SafeAssign is a service that assesses the originality of every outline and manuscript submitted in this class. The service compares "submitted assignments against a pool of academic papers to identify areas of overlap between the submitted assignment and existing works" (http://help.ramct.colostate.edu/safeassign/StudentsandSafeAssign.pdf).You will be required to submit assignments electronically to the service; it is no more difficult than emailing an attachment. **Students who do not submit their assignments to SafeAssign on time will receive a *zero* on their assignment until the matching document is submitted successfully.**

While the instructor will provide detailed instructions for using SafeAssign at the appropriate time, here are a few important points to remember:

- SafeAssign simply assesses originality. In cases of matches to other sources (common in a research-based speech outline), your instructor will assess whether or not proper citation form was employed.

- Be sure you complete your work early enough to deal with unexpected delays in submission. *Failure to post required assignments successfully on SafeAssign may result in a score of zero for the corresponding assignment.*

- In order to protect your privacy, *do not put your name on the electronically submitted paper*; the program will properly link you with your paper internally.

- It is important to understand how the university defines plagiarism—Plagiarism: copying of language, structure, ideas, or thoughts of another, and representing them as one's own without proper acknowledgement (CSU General Catalog 2012–2013, 1.6, page 8, http://catalog.colostate.edu/Content/files/2012/FrontPDF/1.6POLICIES.pdf).

SafeAssign identifies the portion of your work that is original and flags instances of copying. Copying, with proper citation, is not plagiarism. One of the objectives of this course is to teach speakers how to incorporate research into their speeches ethically and effectively, supporting their own analysis with high-quality research.

Honor Pledge:
To assist and remind students, faculty, and other community members that we aspire to form a culture of academic integrity at Colorado State University, students are encouraged to write and/or sign the CSU Honor Pledge on all assignments for this class. The honor pledge is: **"I have not given, received, or used any unauthorized assistance."**

Accommodating Special Needs:
Students who require special accommodations during testing or instruction should first contact Resources for Disabled Students, 100 General Services, Fort Collins, CO 80523, (970) 491-6385 (V/TDD). Information about Resources for Disabled Students can be found online at http://rds.colostate.edu/. The SPCM 200 staff is happy to accommodate the specific needs of our students, provided the policies and procedures outlined by Resources for Disabled Students are followed. Please discuss your needs with your instructor *at the beginning of the semester* so that the requisite accommodations may be put in place. Failure to contact your instructor at the beginning of the semester will not justify retroactive grade changes. Be advised that speech deadlines are firm. A last-minute extension will not be granted.

COURSE SCHEDULES
A general course schedule laying out expected speech days, course readings, and the exam will be distributed by instructors on the first day of class. If students do not receive a course schedule, they should follow up with their instructor immediately. These are general scheduling guidelines and do not reflect specific speech days, assignment due dates, etc. Actual due dates will vary by class due to changing enrollments, snow days, etc. Please follow assigned due dates for all work provided by instructors in class.

SPEECH ASSIGNMENTS*
*Students will have additional assignments and exams in this class besides the speech assignments below. See the grading scale and your instructor's syllabus addendum for further information.

Diagnostic Speech (0 points)
Prepare and present a 2–3 minute speech on a topic specified by your instructor. This speech is designed to "diagnose" your speaking strengths and areas that need improvement. It will be graded on a pass/fail basis. If you attempt to complete the assignment in good faith, **you will pass**.

Informative Speech (100 points)
Prepare and present a 4–6 minute speech that conveys useful or interesting information to an audience. Cite at least 4–6 different *sources* for your audience during the speech (put the names of your sources in parentheses when you cite them within the body of your outline, as well as additional and appropriate citation information), and include *a minimum of one visual aid* prepared specifically for this assignment. Prior to the delivery of the speech, submit one copy of a typed complete-sentence outline, including a works cited page, to your instructor. Upload that identical file (with your name removed) to SafeAssign. Avoid spelling, typographical, or grammatical errors.

Invitational Speech (200 points)
You will prepare a 5–7 minute speech to explore an issue, and then moderate a 3–4 minute dialogue with your class colleagues (maximum of *12 minutes total* for the speech and dialogue). Then you will present a brief conclusion (no more than one minute) summarizing your speech content and dialogue. Your topic should be potentially suitable for the policy speech assignment, and you should use the invitational dialogue as an opportunity to 1) find a topic for your policy speech, and/or 2) gain a greater understanding of and appreciation for your audience's diverse perspectives before you design your policy speech. Cite at least **5–7 different** *sources* for your audience during the speech (put the names of your sources in parentheses when you cite them within the body of your outline). On the day of your dialogues, turn in one copy of a *typed outline* of your invitational speech with *dialogue question prompts* listed at the end and a works cited page. Upload that identical file (with your name removed) to SafeAssign. Avoid spelling, typographical, or grammatical errors.

Policy Speech (250 points)
Prepare and present a 6–8 minute speech that proposes a plan to solve a current public problem. After your 8 minute speech, field 2–3 minutes worth of questions from the audience. You may arrange your policy speech into either the problem-solution organizational pattern or the problem-cause-solution pattern. Make sure to relate your discussion of the problem and proposed solution specifically to your class audience. Cite at least *6–8 different sources* for your audience during the speech (put the names of your sources in parentheses when you cite them within the body of your outline). Prior to the delivery of the speech, submit one copy of a typed complete-sentence outline, including a works cited page to your instructor. Upload that identical file (with your name removed) to SafeAssign. Avoid spelling, typographical, or grammatical errors.

Commemorative Speech (100 points)
Prepare and present a 4–5 minute speech that pays tribute to a person, concept, organization, or institution. This speech will be delivered from manuscript. Organize your speech's main points according to those virtues exhibited by the subject you have chosen to amplify. Incorporate examples of both imagery and rhythm into your speech, and label them on your manuscript. **Be sure to select a topic that is praiseworthy for general audiences** (praising excessive alcohol use or violence are bad topics for general audience, for instance). Making sure your topic is approved by your instructor will ensure you pick an appropriately praiseworthy topic. Prior to the delivery, submit a typed,

double-spaced copy of your manuscript to your instructor. Upload that identical file (with your name removed) to SafeAssign. Avoid spelling, typographical, or grammatical errors.

GRADING STANDARDS

Although each assignment has a distinct set of grading criteria, there are general standards that can be applied to all of the speeches:

The **"B"** or **"A"** speech presents a thesis that is significantly challenging for college students. The analysis reflects superior understanding of the subject and its appropriate development. The central idea is introduced so as to engage the concern as well as the interest of the listener. The organization of main points and supporting materials is strikingly clear. The delivery of the speech is marked by excellent choice of language, articulation, and animation. The speech reflects a high degree of polish as presented in final form. While a "B" speech is above average, an "A" speech is clearly superior in all areas.

The **"C"** speech meets the basic requirements of the assignment. It develops a clearly defined idea that is phrased and presented in a manner significant for the audience. There is supporting material for the main points. The speech has a recognizable developmental pattern. The speaker makes adequate use of basic physical and vocal delivery. The "C" speech is an average speech.

The **"D"** or **"F"** speech treats a topic in a trite or inconsequential way, or it may not conform to the assignment. The thesis may be vague or too broad to cover in the allocated time. There is a lack of structure and often a considerable amount of irrelevant, superficial material. There is little attempt to adapt to the audience and situation. Delivery is broken or lacks variety, and there may be problems with the choice of language. While the "D" speech is below average, it does have some saving grace. The "F" speech has none.

You should understand assignment criteria and your instructor's expectations before you prepare each speech. If you are unclear about assignment specifications, visit with your instructor about your questions and concerns. If you do not understand why you received a particular grade on a speech, schedule an appointment to talk with your instructor. Our goal is to help you become the best speaker you can be. That goal can only be accomplished if 1) the instructor evaluates your work frankly and accurately, and 2) you and your instructor work together to improve your performance. If you discuss problems and concerns with your instructor early in the semester (rather than two weeks before the end of the semester) the chances are greatly improved that this class will be a productive and positive experience for you.

You will be evaluated by the excellence of your work alone. Effort, *per se*, is not a factor in grading.

GRADING SCALE

Below is the point distribution and corresponding letter grade for each assignment in class:

LETTER GRADE	INFORMATIVE	INVITATIONAL	POLICY	COMMEMORATIVE	QUIZZES OR MIDTERM	FINAL EXAM	MISC. (HOMEWORK, PARTICIPATION, ACTIVITIES)
A+	100	200	250	100	100	150	100
A	96	192	240	96	96	144	96
A–	93	186	233	93	93	140	93
B+	89	178	223	89	89	134	89
B	86	172	215	86	86	129	86
B–	83	166	208	83	83	125	83
C+	79	158	198	79	79	119	79
C	76	152	190	76	76	114	76
C–	73	146	183	73	73	110	73
D+	69	138	173	69	69	104	69
D	66	132	165	66	66	99	66
D–	63	126	158	63	63	95	63
F	59 and below	118 and below	148 and below	59 and below	59 and below	89 and below	59 and below

Here is the 1000-point scale we will use to assign final course grades:

1000–933	A
932–900	A–
899–867	B+
866–833	B
832–800	B–
799–767	C+
766–700	C
699–600	D
599 and below	F

GRADE RECORD

This sheet can serve as a record of the due dates for each major assignment and grades you earn throughout the semester. Fill in the *number of points* you earn as you complete each assignment.

Diagnostic   Date: _____   Grade: _Pass/Fail_

Informative   Date: _____   Grade: _____

Invitational   Date: _____   Grade: _____

Policy   Date: _____   Grade: _____

Commemorative   Date: _____   Grade: _____

Homework, etc.

Grade: _____

Quizzes/Midterm

Grade: _____

Final Exam   Grade: _____

TOTAL: _____

To determine your overall grade, compare the points you have earned with the grading scale on the previous page. During the semester, you can add the points you have earned and divide it by the total points possible for the assignments completed.

UNIT 1

INTRODUCTION TO SPEAKING

Reading: *Invitation to Public Speaking*, Ch. 1–3

Unit Objectives: Upon completion of this unit, you should understand:

- the power and influence of public speaking

- the public speaking process

- when and why we speak in public

- how to overcome nervousness in public speaking

- the connection between listening and creating community

- why we sometimes fail to listen

- how to listen effectively and ethically

Assignment: Diagnostic Speech

Prepare and present a 2–3 minute speech on a topic specified by your instructor. This speech is designed to "diagnose" your speaking strengths and areas that need improvement. It will be graded on a pass/fail basis. If you attempt to complete the assignment in good faith, ***you will pass***.

The Diagnostic Speech Assignment Emphasizes the Following Skills:

- **Organization:** Make sure your speech has an identifiable introduction, body, and conclusion.

- **Extemporaneous Delivery:** Engage your audience with a dynamic speaking style and sustained eye contact. Deliver the speech from a "bare bones" outline on index cards.

- **Time Management:** Practice your speech so that you conform to the time limit. This is probably the most important rule. If several students take more than 3 minutes, there will not be enough class time for everyone to speak.

Tips and Suggestions: Organizing Your First Speech

Even a short speech should follow sound organizational principles. Make sure your diagnostic speech has an identifiable introduction, body, and conclusion. Use each section of the speech to accomplish the following specific goals.

Introduction

- *Attention-Getter:* Begin by gaining the audience's attention and getting them interested in your topic. Start with a short story, an interesting question, a unique fact—something that will grab audience members and compel them to listen to you.

- *Thesis and Preview:* Reveal your speech topic, the purpose of your speech, and preview your main points.

Body

- Organize the body of your speech into distinct main points. Don't just lump all the information together. Divide it according to topics and make choices about what you should include and what you should leave out of the speech.

Conclusion

- *Review:* Briefly summarize the main points you covered in the speech.

- *"When to Clap" Line:* Audiences need a signal that the speech has ended and they can clap. Plan a specific closing line for your speech that lets your audience know, definitively, that you're done. Try to make it more creative than "Thank you," "That's all," or "I'm done."

Good organization enhances your credibility, makes your speeches clear and interesting, and helps you accomplish your communication goals. Start practicing the basics of organization now.

Why It Is Important: Index Cards

Putting your speaking notes on index cards rather than sheets of paper helps improve your delivery in a number of ways:

- Key words and phrases fit on an index card, but your whole speech won't. Index cards help you create good speaker's notes.

- Since index cards are small and sturdy you can hold them and still move away from the podium a bit to incorporate movement into your speech. Remember, in many speaking situations, you will not have a lectern to stand behind or a podium to put your notes on!

Tip: Number your index cards so that you can easily verify they are complete and in the correct order. Cards can get mixed up or dropped if you're not careful.

Speaker _____

Topic _____

Unit 1

DIAGNOSTIC SPEECH

+ Excellent   ✓ **Satisfactory**   **-- Needs improvement**   **0 Failed to complete**

INTRODUCTION
Captured audience attention   _____
Previewed main points   _____

BODY
Main points clear   _____
Main points developed   _____

CONCLUSION
Signaled start of conclusion   _____
Reviewed main points   _____
Decisive/artistic last line   _____

DELIVERY
Maintained eye contact   _____
Used vocal variety   _____
Projected adequately   _____
Pronunciation correct   _____
Articulation clear   _____
Rate appropriate   _____
Paused effectively   _____
Gestures purposeful   _____
Mannerisms appropriate   _____
Facial expression   _____
Spoke fluently   _____
Extemporaneous style   _____
Effective use of speaking notes   _____

ADDITIONAL ITEMS
Completed in time limit   _____
Topic appropriate   _____
Fulfilled assignment requirements   _____

Specific strengths and areas for improvement:

CRITIQUE SHEET

Instructor comments and suggestions:

Time: _____

Grade: __Pass/Fail__

Name_____

Topic_____

Unit 1

DIAGNOSTIC SPEECH

1. After viewing your video or thinking about your speech experience, identify your speaking strengths and areas for improvement as they appeared in your diagnostic speech.

2. Specifically, what speech-related skills would you like to improve upon throughout the semester?

3. In terms of preparation and practice, what will you need to do differently for your next speech in this class to improve your performance?

SELF-EVALUATION SHEET

4. What are some of the fears you have related to public speaking?

5. What do you hope to take from this class to use in your future communication experiences?

UNIT 2

INFORMATIVE SPEAKING

Reading: *Invitation to Public Speaking*, Ch. 4–8, 10–12

Unit Objectives: Upon completion of this unit, you should understand:

- how to select a topic and purpose

- guidelines and organizational principles of informative speaking

- how to begin and end your speech

- the different types of outlines and how to prepare them

- how to incorporate quality supporting materials into your speech

- how to design and use visual aids

Assignment: Informative Speech

Prepare and present a 4–6 minute speech that conveys useful or interesting information to an audience. Cite at least 4–6 different *sources* for your audience during the speech (put the names of your sources in parentheses when you cite them within the body of your outline, as well as additional and appropriate citation information), and include *a minimum of one visual aid* prepared specifically for this assignment. Prior to the delivery of the speech, submit one copy of a typed complete-sentence outline, including a works cited page, to your instructor. Upload that identical file (with your name removed) to SafeAssign. *Students who do not submit to SafeAssign may receive a zero on their speech.* Avoid spelling, typographical, or grammatical errors.

The Informative Speech Assignment Emphasizes the Following Skills:

- **Organization:** Focus on clarity in this speech. Your speech should have a well-developed introduction, distinct and logical main points, transitions between points, and a concise, compelling conclusion.

- **Research:** This will be your first research-based speech of the semester. You should not only find a variety of credible sources and interesting supporting material, but you also must cite your sources clearly for the audience.

- **Outlining:** A well-prepared complete-sentence outline will enable you to fulfill the organizational and research requirements of this assignment. Make sure you follow the outlining models in this *Coursebook* carefully.

- **Visual Support:** This assignment allows you to practice two skills related to visual support: 1) preparing professional-quality visual aids, and 2) using them in a way that enhances (rather than detracts from) your credibility.

- **Speaker Credibility:** Every aspect of your performance, from topic selection to research to delivery, should evidence your personal credibility as a speaker.

- **Audience Adaptation:** Prepare your speech with your specific audience in mind. Devise strategies to give them useful information, keep them interested, and adapt to their knowledge of your topic.

Tips and Suggestions: Choosing a Topic For Your Informative Speech

When you choose your topic for the Informative Speech, make sure it passes the *"Hmmm, that's interesting. I didn't know that"* test. That's what you want your audience to be thinking after your speech. Many topics pass one part of the test, but your topic should pass both. For example, you could do a speech on how microprocessors function. Most people don't know much about that, but it's probably not an interesting speech either. Conversely, you might think that describing your favorite sport or hobby is interesting, but unless you find a truly unique angle, most people already know a lot about many popular sports and hobbies. So, while you should choose a topic to which you have a personal connection, you'll need to do research to find unique information that your audience is likely to find new and interesting.

Why It Is Important: Complete-Sentence Outlining

Complete-Sentence Outline

I. Introduction
    A. Attention-getter
    B. Audience adaptation
    C. Credibility
    D. Thesis

Transition

II. Main point one
    A. Subpoint
       1) Support

The outline has several functions:

First, it helps you prepare your speech. Before we required complete-sentence outlines, students would put off preparing for their speech, run out of time, and come to class unprepared. They would give disorganized, poorly researched, impromptu speeches. Grades actually improved after we instituted an outlining requirement because students were forced to develop main points and support each point with evidence in advance.

Second, the outline format helps you organize your speech. The reason you don't just write it in paragraph form is because we want you to think in terms of breaking your speech up into main points, supporting each point with evidence, having a distinct introduction and conclusion, and separating each point with connectives. The outline format helps you visualize the proper organization for a speech.

From a teaching perspective, the outline helps your instructor to provide you with better feedback. If a point is unclear in your speech, or a transition is poorly worded, they can respond specifically on your outline to what went wrong and how to improve it. If all they have is phrases on the outline, they cannot be as specific in their feedback and you're more likely to repeat the mistake on your next speech.

When you're preparing your complete sentence outline, refer to the models in this coursebook. Be sure to include the entire text of your speech in outline form, label key introduction elements, transitions, and conclusion elements, underline or highlight your sources, and upload a file identical to your instructor's hard copy to SafeAssign.

Why It Is Important: Time Management

Everyone has time constraints. If your employer asks you to stay beyond your regular shift at work, you might expect overtime pay. If a meeting runs longer than the end time promised on the agenda, people will become impatient. We expect our television programs to begin and end precisely as stated in the published schedule—otherwise our programmed recording might miss some of the show. If a friend habitually shows up late for plans you've made, it could put a strain on the friendship. And we all know what happens when an instructor fails to adjourn class promptly.

Similarly, you have time constraints in your public speaking class. Time limits for each speech assignment will vary, and although you may not think so now, it is far more common for students to exceed the maximum time limits for a speech than it is to fail to fulfill the minimum requirement. Limiting your speech to the time allotted requires you to adequately narrow the scope of your topic, edit your speech carefully, and practice repeatedly.

If speakers routinely speak beyond the maximum time limit, their classmates suffer negative consequences—either having their own time constrained or missing their assigned speaking day all together. This is not fair to your classmates and it does not help you prepare for the standards of timeliness you will face after graduation. Additionally, an important skill that public speakers must possess is the ability to edit their presentation to meet existing time limits—which often are imposed by someone other than the speaker. Consequently, failure to conform to time limits in this class will negatively affect your grade. In order to avoid this unpleasant consequence, keep your speech tightly focused, limit the amount of information you intend to cover, follow a clear structure, and practice, practice, practice.

Tips and Suggestions: Research at Colorado State University

by Naomi Lederer

Researching a speech is like researching any other project. Read the suggestions found on the next few pages and make use of the Web pages referred to which recommend strategies and sources to use. The Library Guide created specifically for this course was designed in consultation with the Director of the SPCM 200 course, so you can use it with confidence.

TIPS FOR RESEARCHING IN THE LIBRARY

1. **Ask for help:** There is a service point in the library with staff to assist you. The primary location for research assistance is the Help Desk.

2. **Plan ahead:** Give yourself enough time—as in *hours*—to do your research. A speech researched in an hour or less is going to be noticeably lacking in depth and thoughtfulness. In addition, if you do your research just before a project is due, you won't have any time to *think* about the information you have found before you write about it.

3. **Finding your way around:** Visit the library and get oriented to the layout and services of the building before you need to do research. The library Web site offers resources to help you navigate the space, including maps and directions at < http://lib.colostate.edu/about/locations>.

CHOOSING A TOPIC

Don't lock onto a topic until you know you can find enough—and the right kind—of information about it. You are doing current topics, and there is not going to be much information available for some subjects. By changing or adapting your topic near the beginning of your research, you don't waste time. Look for articles in the recommended databases (and print indexes), and if you don't find at least five useful and available articles after looking through four or five databases and indexes (don't give up after only one or two), *change* (or adapt) your topic!

A list of recommended databases and indexes can be found on the SPCM 200 guide on the Libraries' Web site (see URL under SPCM 200 Library Guide below). Look for the "Articles" tab. A number of the databases, useful for current topics, have full text (complete articles) online. Use FindIt@CSU when the full text is not immediately available.

Having difficulty choosing a topic? Look for suggestions on "Topic Selection Tips" at: <http://lib. colostate.edu/howto/toptip.html>

SPCM 200 LIBRARY GUIDE

The library guide designed specifically for this course has useful information such as recommended reference books, Web pages, and databases. The pages can be found at: <http://libguides.colostate. edu/spcm200>. The guide lists useful resources for your research. Select the tab(s) most relevant to your current assignment and return regularly.

LIBRARY RESOURCES

There are many reference materials available on the Web. However, there still are thousands of useful books in the reference collection, so don't overlook them!

- **General encyclopedias** are useful for background information. The following Web site has a list of general encyclopedias found in Morgan Library: <http://lib.colostate.edu/howto/genency. html>. Scroll down to see the links to encyclopedias freely available on the Web.

- **Subject encyclopedias** are useful for specialized and more technical descriptions. A list of recommended titles is available at: <http://lib.colostate.edu/howto/encyclo.html>. These titles are listed by subject area; for example, societal, environment, and health.

- **Statistical sources** can provide valuable information that can support your argument. See a list of useful resources with statistics at <http://lib.colostate.edu/howto/stats.html> and <http:// libguides.colostate.edu/statisticalsources>.

- **Government documents** should not be overlooked. For unbiased research on contemporary topics, see *CQ Researcher* found online through the Articles & Databases page. See *Congressional Quarterly Weekly Report*, also found online. Be certain that you access these through the CSU Library gateway (Articles & Databases or from the Library Catalog) or you will not be able to use them.

You can identify books (both print and electronic), government documents, microforms, journals, films, and more in the library catalog, Sage (http://catalog.library.colostate.edu/), and Discovery (http://discovery.library.colostate.edu/). Check the status for availability of print titles. Write down the call number and the location for each item—then if you need directions, a staff member can assist you quickly.

HOW TO FIND ARTICLES IN JOURNALS AND MAGAZINES

Finding articles is a five-step process. Follow the steps in sequence, and, if necessary, ask for help at the Help Desk.

Step 1: *Select Indexes.*
Use lists found on the SPCM 200 library guide or ask a for a reference librarian to give you suggestions. Help Desk staff can refer you to the subject specialist for your topic.

Step 2: *Search for the Topic.*
Have different variations of terms in mind (a.k.a. different ways of saying the same thing). You might call the topic "biodiversity" or "fútbol," but if the index uses "diversity biology" or "soccer" you will miss relevant sources!

Step 3: *Interpret the Information in the Index.*
Identify the Author, "Title of the Article." *Journal/Magazine Title* volume (date): and pages.

Step 4: *Determine if the Libraries Own the Journal.*
Details on how to do this are available at <http://lib.colostate.edu/howto/owns.html>. Write down the call number and the location (may vary by volume/year/issue) of the journal that the article is in. Use FindIt@CSU when it is available.

Step 5: *Locate the Journal and Find the Article in It.*
Is the journal in the Journal Room (journals shelved in call number order), on microfiche or microfilm, in the moveable shelves, in storage, or even linked directly from the library catalog? You may want to request the article from Interlibrary Loan if CSU does not own it and it appears useful.

Do your research as soon as possible so you have enough time to gather your materials.

If in Step 3 you discover that the article is full text online, you don't need to do steps 4 or 5—unless there are images or tables you wish to see that aren't shown. You will still need the article's bibliographical information for your bibliography or works cited list.

EVALUATE SOURCES

It is critical that you evaluate the materials that you find. Inaccurate or misleading sources are useful to you as sources to criticize ONLY if you are aware that they are inaccurate and misleading! Use the evaluation tools listed below to help you determine *if* and *how* you want to use a resource.

How to Evaluate Books	http://lib.colostate.edu/howto/evalbk.html
How to Evaluate Journal Articles	http://lib.colostate.edu/howto/evaljrl.html
How to Evaluate a Web Page	http://lib.colostate.edu/howto/evalweb.html
How to Evaluate a a Movie, Video, or Film Clip	http://lib.colostate.edu/howto/evalmovie.html

TIPS FOR FINDING MATERIALS ON THE WEB

The Web is a useful resource for current topics. The recommended sources on the SPCM 200 guide have links to newspapers and other useful Web sites. Make use of these.

If you wish to seek out information on the Web:

- Be aware of homographs—words spelled the same that mean something different. For example, "Mercury" can mean the god, the element, or the planet.

- Use advanced techniques when available. Look for advanced searching tips under "Help," "Advanced Searching," or "Searching Tips" on browser home pages.

- Use quotes around phrases. For example, "Rocky Mountain National Park."

- Use Boolean logic (AND, OR) when available. The browser may refer to these as "all" (AND) or "any" (OR) of the words. For a detailed explanation of Boolean logic, see <http://lib.colostate.edu/howto/others/boolean.html>.

Current information is going to be found on news sites such as newspapers, television, and radio stations. Links to a number of news sites are on <http://lib.colostate.edu/howto/late.html>. When you find information on one of these sites and if you think an article might be important, *print it out immediately*! News sites are updated constantly, and current news articles can disappear at any time—or may only be available for a fee. A Web address for a news site saved for a week—or even a day—frequently has entirely different content by the time you get back to it.

ADDITIONAL STRATEGIES

- Once you find a useful article, use it to identify additional articles. See "Finding Articles on Similar Topics" for suggestions at <http://lib.colostate.edu/howto/simtop.html>.

- Figure out what type of journal your article is in by using the "Popular Magazines vs. Trade Magazines vs. Scholarly Journals" chart found on <http://lib.colostate.edu/howto/poplr.html>. For an article you found online, use "Evaluation Clues for Articles Found on the Web or in Library Databases" <http://lib.colostate.edu/howto/evalclues.html>.

- Interviewing an expert or other knowledgeable person can be an excellent way to gather current information. Read "Interviews" for suggestions on how to identify someone to interview and to find out how to prepare for the interview at <http://lib.colostate.edu/howto/others/intervw.html>.

POINT OF VIEW

Be sure to get as many different points of view as possible. Use articles from different journals and Web sites. Be careful; some organizations sponsor both journals and Web pages.

Creating the Works Cited Page

by Thomas R. Dunn and Jennifer Emerling Bone

This information is based on MLA style, taken in part from Purdue University's Online Writing Lab (OWL) at <http://owl.english.purdue.edu/owl/>. It reflects the expectations for a Works Cited page as established in the *MLA Handbook for Writers of Research Papers* (7th ed.) and the *MLA Style Manual and Guide to Scholarly Publishing* (3rd ed.).

- Begin on a NEW sheet of paper.

- Sources in the work cited page are ***always*** alphabetized ***regardless*** of the type of source. **Do not** label or categorize the type of source used.

- List only sources that are cited in the speech.

- Double-space each entry.

- Indent additional lines of the same source five spaces.

BOOK
Author's Last Name, Author's First Name. *Title of the Book*. City of Publication: Publisher, Year of Publication. Medium of Publication.

Butler, Judith. *Gender Trouble: Feminism and the Subversion of Identity*. New York: Routledge, 1999. Print.

BOOK BY MULTIPLE AUTHORS
List the names of the book's authors in the order in which they appear on the title page of the book. Reverse the name of ONLY the first author. Then, follow the above guidelines.

First Author's Last Name, First Author's First Name, Second Author's First Name and Last Name, and Third Author's First Name and Last Name. *Title of the Book*. City of Publication: Publisher, Year of Publication. Medium of Publication.

Golden, James L., Goodwin Berquist, William Coleman, and James M. Sproule. *The Rhetoric of Western Thought: From the Mediterranean World to the Global Setting*. Dubuque, IA: Kendall Hunt, 2011. Print.

AN EDITED BOOK, ANTHOLOGY, OR COLLECTION
Use for a book which features essays by other authors.

First Author's Last Name, First Author's First Name, Second Author's First Name and Last Name, and Third Author's First Name and Last Name, eds. *Title of the Book*. City of Publication: Publisher, Year of Publication. Medium of Publication.

Dickinson, Greg, Carole Blair, and Brian L. Ott, eds. *Places of Public Memory: The Rhetoric of Museums and Memorials*. Tuscaloosa: University of Alabama Press, 2010. Print.

UNKNOWN AUTHOR

Begin with the title, but do not use A, An, or The as the starting word when you alphabetize entries.

Title of the Work. City of Publication: Publisher, Year of Publication. Medium of Publication.

The Pocket Oxford Spanish Dictionary. Oxford: Oxford UP, 1997. Print.

ARTICLES IN A MAGAZINE OR NEWSPAPER

Author(s). "Title of Article." *Title of Periodical or Newspaper* Day Month Year: Pages. Medium of Publication.

Sang-Hun, Choe. "North Korea Declares 1953 War Truce Nullified." *New York Times* 11 March 2013: A1. Online.

ARTICLE OR ESSAY IN A SCHOLARLY JOURNAL

Author(s). "Title of Journal Article." *Title of the Journal* Volume.Issue Number (Year): pages. Medium of Publication.

Ott, Brian L. and Eric Aoki. "The Politics of Negotiating Public Tragedy: Media Framing of the Matthew Shepard Murder." *Rhetoric & Public Affairs* 5.3 (2002): 483–505. Print.

PERSONAL INTERVIEW

Used when you cite an interview that you conducted. Published interviews are cited differently.

Last name of interviewee, First name of interviewee. Personal Interview. Day Month Year of Interview.

Anderson, Karrin. Personal Interview. 5 Mar. 2012.

FILM OR MOVIE

Film name. Dir. Director's First name Last name. Distributor, Year of Release. Medium of Publication.

An Inconvenient Truth. Dir. Robert Kenner. Paramount Vantage, 2006. DVD.

WEB SITE

URLs are no longer required in MLA citations. However, if your instructor requires them, place the URL after the date of access. Use the abbreviation "n.d." to indicate no creation date was given and "n.p." to indicate no publisher or sponsor was given.

Editor or Author. Name of Site. Publisher or Sponsor of the Site, Date of Creation or Upload. Medium of Publication. Date of Access.

"About Our Research." American Heart Association, 2013. Web. 11 Mar. 2013.

EXAMPLE OF A WORKS CITED PAGE

Remember to alphabetize all your sources and start the Works Cited on a separate page of your outline. Start the Works Cited at the top of the page.

Works Cited

"About Our Research." American Heart Association, 2013. Web. 11 Mar. 2013.

Anderson, Karrin. Personal Interview. 5 Mar. 2012.

An Inconvenient Truth. Dir. Robert Kenner. Paramount Vantage, 2006. DVD.

Butler, Judith. *Gender Trouble: Feminism and the Subversion of Identity*. New York: Routledge, 1999. Print.

Dickinson, Greg, Carole Blair, and Brian L. Ott, eds. *Places of Public Memory: The Rhetoric of Museums and Memorials*. Tuscaloosa: University of Alabama Press, 2010. Print.

Golden, James L., Goodwin Berquist, William Coleman, and James M. Sproule. *The Rhetoric of Western Thought: From the Mediterranean World to the Global Setting*. Dubuque, IA: Kendall Hunt, 2011. Print.

Ott, Brian L. and Eric Aoki. "The Politics of Negotiating Public Tragedy: Media Framing of the Matthew Shepard Murder." *Rhetoric & Public Affairs* 5.3 (2002): 483–505. Print.

The Pocket Oxford Spanish Dictionary. Oxford: Oxford UP, 1997. Print.

Sang-Hun, Choe. "North Korea Declares 1953 War Truce Nullified." *New York Times* 11 March 2013: A1. Online.

PITFALLS OF POWERPOINT *AND HOW TO AVOID THEM!*

Computer-generated visual support (PowerPoint, Keynote, Prezi, etc.) is a widely used and frequently abused technology. It can be a wonderful aid to public speakers but also has the potential to detract from your oral performance if used improperly. The following tips and suggestions will enable you to use computer-aided visual support in a productive way.

COMMON DESIGN PITFALLS

✖ **Too much:** Too much of a good thing can turn into a bad thing. Just because your software allows you to introduce motion, sound effects, multiple backgrounds, and hidden slides doesn't mean you should give in to the temptation. If your slides are too busy they might confuse or distract the audience. If they are noisy, they'll take the focus off you as a speaker. If they contain multiple hidden slides it will be easy for you to get off track during the presentation. *Remember the basic rule of VA design: Keep It Simple!*

✖ **Too wordy:** Your instructor likely uses PowerPoint to display outlines of class lectures with key terms and definitions. But class lectures have different goals than public speeches. In class, you need to be able to copy down exact terms and definitions. In a public speaking context, visual aids should enhance the clarity and interest value of your speech. They should be *visual **not** verbal* media. **Do not** simply display an outline of your speech for the class. Instead, use the computer to put up graphics, design charts and graphs, and even include short audio or video clips if appropriate for your topic.

✖ **Too advanced:** We try to keep our classroom equipment up to date, but this is (after all) a state university. We don't always have the most memory, the fastest processors, or the latest version of software. If your graphics are too large they may not load. If your presentation was prepared on a later version of the software, text and images may display differently (or not at all). If you're counting on a specific media player, it might not be loaded on the classroom computer. *Always check out a few sample slides the class period before you speak to ensure that our technology is compatible with your presentation.*

COMMON PRESENTATION PITFALLS

✖ **Too dark:** It is common to turn out the lights when using projected visual aids, but that leads the audience to focus on the slides, not the speaker. *Choose a background that will display in a fully lit room.*

✖ **Too technological:** Technology can be a useful and inexpensive way to display key information for your audience: a graphic you downloaded from a Web site or a chart you designed to help your audience visualize the impact of your statistics. Just because you use PowerPoint, however, does not mean that you need a slide for every moment in your speech. Put up a few key images, insert blank slides in between so the images are not up longer than they need to be, and leave it at that. *You want the audience's focus to stay on you, the speaker.*

✖ **Too distracted:** If you haven't practiced with your presentation, you often can get wrapped up in making it work during the speech. You focus intently on the keyboard, or turn your back on your audience and talk to the screen. Instead, *design a simple presentation that is easy to manage during your speech.* When you want to point to something specific on screen, step back, keep your shoulders facing the audience, and gesture broadly to the image. *Your integration of technology should be as seamless as your speech transitions.*

GENERAL RULE

Let the technology support the speaker, not dominate the speech!

Sample Informative Speech Outline
for Analysis and Discussion

SPCM 200, [Section]
[Date]

Dark Chocolate

by Hannah Huntington, SPCM 200 student

Specific Purpose Statement: To inform my audience about the history and health benefits of dark chocolate

Thesis: The health benefits of dark chocolate began as beliefs in ancient history, are currently supported by health research and studies, and could be a significant part of the future of health, dark chocolate, and the chocolate industry.

Pattern of Organization: Chronological

Introduction

I. [*Attention-Getter*] By a show of hands, how many of you like chocolate? Keep your hands raised if you have indulged in this sweet at some point during the last week.

II. [*Reveal topic and relate to audience*] As I have just shown you, the majority of people enjoy chocolate.

   A. According to the National Confectioners Association (NCA), the majority of Americans like chocolate, with almost half of the population consuming this sweet confection every day (NCA).

   B. My guess is that while many of you enjoy common kinds of chocolate, dark chocolate may be an unfamiliar taste.

III. [*Establish credibility*] I am a dark-chocoholic.

   A. I was introduced to real dark chocolate while living overseas in Europe.

   B. Since then, I have been hooked on this rich yet bittersweet treat.

   C. Over the past few years, dark chocolate has become an increasingly popular subject, spawning extensive health research that suggests dark chocolate is beneficial to one's health.

   D. As a consumer, I have become interested in all that dark chocolate has to offer and have looked to the research literature for answers about its health benefits.

IV. [*Thesis and Preview*] Today I will share with you a brief history of dark chocolate and health, what current research findings suggest about its health benefits, and what the future looks like for this decadent sweet.

Signpost: First, let's step back and unwrap the rich history of dark chocolate.

Body

I. According to the Smithsonian, historians estimate that chocolate has been around for at least 2,000 years (Bensen).

    A. In order to understand the history of dark chocolate, it is important to understand a few things about chocolate itself.

        1. The National Confectioners Association states that chocolate is made from beans harvested from the cocoa tree (NCA).

        2. The beans are enclosed in what is known as a cocoa pod.

        3. Once removed from the pod, the cocoa beans can be used.

        4. Dark chocolate is cocoa that contains little or no sugar and no milk and is bitter and strong in flavor (NCA).

    B. The Smithsonian suggests cocoa beans were used first by the Ancient Mayans and Aztecs (Bensen).

        1. Both ancient tribes worshipped the cocoa beans, referring to them as "the food of the gods" (Bensen).

        2. They didn't use the beans to make chocolate in the way we do today.

        3. Instead, they ground up the beans and mixed in spices and water to form a dark chocolate drink; thus dark chocolate was born (Bensen).

    C. Even during these ancient times, dark chocolate was perceived to have health benefits.

        1. An article in the *Chicago Tribune* credits the Mayans with discovering the potential health benefits of cocoa and dark chocolate (Zanteson).

            a. As mentioned before, the Mayans believed that cocoa beans were powerful and contained many healing properties (Bensen).

            b. They would use the chocolate liquid for medicine (Zanteson).

            c. This same source suggests that the Mayans believed cocoa beans could help the heart and help to relieve depression (Zanteson).

        2. As centuries passed, dark chocolate continued to be consumed as a drink, "believed to have nutritious [and] medicinal…properties" (Bensen).

    D. However, by the 19th century, dark chocolate was completely transformed into the solid bars we are all so familiar with yet it was still believed to hone health benefits (Bensen).

[Visual aid: Dark chocolate bar]

Transition: Now that we've heard about the ancient history behind dark chocolate and its perceived health benefits, let's get a taste of what current research suggests about this sweet.

II. Despite the bad reputation chocolate gets today, research shows that dark chocolate is beneficial to people's health.

    A. In a study done by Andrew Waterhouse, significant amounts of the antioxidants, flavonols, were found in dark chocolate.

        1. These specific antioxidants are said to prevent bad cholesterol from clogging arteries in the body and improve heart health (Chocolate: Food of the Gods).

        2. Waterhouse also found that the higher the percentage of cocoa that is in the dark chocolate, the more flavonol antioxidants it contains, and the more beneficial it is for heart health (Chocolate Health).

    B. In another study, published in the *US National Library of Medicine*, Dr. R. Latif found similar results to that of the study mentioned previously (Latif).

        1. A large scale study mentioned in Latif's work showed that people who ate dark chocolate regularly over a 15 year time span or even a 15 day time span had significantly lower blood pressure that those who did not (Latif).

    C. Current studies also suggest that dark chocolate can be beneficial to the reduction of BMI.

        1. A study published in the Archives of Internal Medicine suggests people who eat dark chocolate have lower BMI (Pearson).

            a. This study found that people who consumed dark chocolate more frequently and consistently had overall, lower BMI.

        2. This finding is fairly new, and it has been mentioned that further research needs to be done in the future (Pearson).

    D. Current studies also suggest that dark chocolate can improve cognitive functions such as memory and mood.

        1. According to an article in the *Chicago Tribune*, dark chocolate can help sustain memory because of the flavonol antioxidant it contains (Zanteson)

            a. These flavonols are absorbed into learning and memory oriented brain areas and have been shown to have a protective effect against cognitive decline (Zanteson).

        2. This research also states that dark chocolate can improve mood, easing symptoms of anxiety and depression (Zanteson).

Internal Summary and Transition: We've heard about the history behind dark chocolate health and the health findings from current research. Now let's take a quick look at what the future may look like for this sweet.

III. The current knowledge of the benefits of dark chocolate could pave the way for a rewardingly bright future.

    A. Many studies I have discussed note that future research should consider other potential health benefits this antioxidant rich food could contain.

        1. With many surprising health benefits already known, benefits of dark chocolate could be limitless.

        2. Fairly recently, PR Newswire released an article stating European chocolate industries are wanting to print health benefits on dark chocolate labels (Chocolate Health).

    B. As the interest in dark chocolate increases, research will continue, discovery will further, and the chocolate industry as we know it may change.

Conclusion

I. [*Signal End*] As we've seen today…

II. [*Review*] …dark chocolate has a rich history, has more recently been found to provide many health benefits, and has a promising future driven by research and health findings.

III. [*Closing Line*] I encourage you to try a piece of dark chocolate and see what differences it can make in your life.

[visual aid: hand out a piece of dark chocolate to everyone]

[page break between speech and works cited page]

Works Cited

Bensen, Amanda. "A Brief History of Chocolate." *Smithsonian.* The Smithsonian, 1 Mar. 2008. Web. 15 Feb. 2014. <http://www.smithsonianmag.com/arts-culture/a-brief-history-of-chocolate-21860917/>.

"Chocolate: Food of the Gods." Chocolate. Yale-New Haven Hospital, n.d. Web. 15 Feb. 2014. <http://www.ynhh.org/about-us/chocolate.aspx>.

"Chocolate Health Claims Under Review for Use on Product Labels." -- *EAST ISLIP, N.Y., Sept. 27, 2012 /PRNewswire/* --. PR Newswire, 27 Sept. 2012. Web. 16 Feb. 2014. <http://www.prnewswire.com/news-releases/chocolate-health-claims-under-review-for-use-on-product-labels-171515791.html>.

Latif, R. "Chocolate/cocoa and Human Health: A Review." *The Netherlands Journal of Medicine* 71.2 (2013): n. pag. *US National Library of Medicine National Institutes of Health.* Web. 16 Feb. 2014. <http://www.njmonline.nl/getpdf.php?id=10000925>.

"NCA Sweet Insights." National Confectioners Association, n.d. Web. 15 Feb. 2014. <http://www.candyusa.com/files/SweetInsights/NCA%20Sweet%20Insights%20-%20Chocolate%20Consumer%20-%20Final.pdf>.

Pearson, Catherine. "Chocolate Eating Linked To Lower BMI." *The Huffington Post.* TheHuffingtonPost.com, 26 Mar. 2012. Web. 16 Feb. 2014. <http://www.huffingtonpost.com/2012/03/26/chocolate-eating-lower-bmi-body-mass-index_n_1379368.html>.

Zanteson, Lori. "Dark Chocolate Can Be a Healthy Treat." *Chicago Tribune*, 19 March 2014. Web. 15 Feb. 2014 < http://www.chicagotribune.com/health/sns-201403181330--tms--premhnstr--k-e20140319-20140319,0,4336276.story>.

Note: The reason that we want you to put your sources in parentheses upon first reference is to highlight their use and make it easier for you and your instructor to identify them in the outline.

UNIT 2 INFORMATIVE SPEAKING

Speaker _____

Topic _____ ~~Vote~~ ~~St~~ _____

Unit 2

INFORMATIVE SPEECH

+ Excellent   **✓ Satisfactory**   **-- Needs improvement**   **0 Failed to complete**

INTRODUCTION		***Specific strengths and areas for improvement:***
Gained audience attention	_____	
Established credibility	_____	
Introduced topic clearly	_____	
Related topic to audience	_____	
Concise thesis/preview	_____	
BODY: ORGANIZATION		
Main points were clear	_____	
Ordered main points logically	_____	
Effective connectives	_____	
BODY: RESEARCH		
Main points fully supported	_____	
Adequate variety of sources	_____	
Used credible sources	_____	
Cited sources orally	_____	
CONCLUSION		
Signaled end of speech	_____	
Summarized main points	_____	
Ended with artistic last line	_____	
DELIVERY		
Maintained eye contact	_____	
Used vocal variety	_____	
Projected adequately	_____	
Pronunciation correct	_____	
Articulation clear	_____	
Rate appropriate	_____	
Paused effectively	_____	
Gestures purposeful	_____	
Proxemics effective	_____	
Mannerisms appropriate	_____	
Facial expression	_____	
Spoke fluently	_____	
Extemporaneous style	_____	
Effective use of speaking notes	_____	

CRITIQUE SHEET

VISUAL AIDS
Clear and easy to see   _____
Professionally designed   _____
Incorporated well into speech   _____
Used technology appropriately   _____
Added clarity to content   _____

OUTLINE
Complete sentence format   _____
Logical subordination   _____
Labels included   _____
Works Cited page   _____
Accurate spelling   _____
Correct grammar   _____
Free of typos/errors   _____

ADDITIONAL ITEMS
Topic challenging   _____
Topic interesting   _____
Topic unique   _____
Adapted to audience   _____
Completed in time limit   _____
Fulfilled assignment
   requirements   _____

Instructor comments and suggestions:

SafeAssign? Y / N

Time: _____

Score: _____ /100

Speaker _____

Topic _____

Unit 2

INFORMATIVE SPEECH

+ Excellent   **✓ Satisfactory**   **-- Needs improvement**   **0 Failed to complete**

INTRODUCTION   *Specific strengths and areas for improvement:*
Gained audience attention   _____
Established credibility   _____
Introduced topic clearly   _____
Related topic to audience   _____
Concise thesis/preview   _____

BODY: ORGANIZATION
Main points were clear   _____
Ordered main points logically   _____
Effective connectives   _____

BODY: RESEARCH
Main points fully supported   _____
Adequate variety of sources   _____
Used credible sources   _____
Cited sources orally   _____

CONCLUSION
Signaled end of speech   _____
Summarized main points   _____
Ended with artistic last line   _____

DELIVERY
Maintained eye contact   _____
Used vocal variety   _____
Projected adequately   _____
Pronunciation correct   _____
Articulation clear   _____
Rate appropriate   _____
Paused effectively   _____
Gestures purposeful   _____
Proxemics effective   _____
Mannerisms appropriate   _____
Facial expression   _____
Spoke fluently   _____
Extemporaneous style   _____
Effective use of speaking notes _____

CRITIQUE SHEET

VISUAL AIDS

Clear and easy to see   _____

Professionally designed   _____

Incorporated well into speech   _____

Used technology appropriately   _____

Added clarity to content   _____

OUTLINE

Complete sentence format   _____

Logical subordination   _____

Labels included   _____

Works Cited page   _____

Accurate spelling   _____

Correct grammar   _____

Free of typos/errors   _____

ADDITIONAL ITEMS

Topic challenging   _____

Topic interesting   _____

Topic unique   _____

Adapted to audience   _____

Completed in time limit   _____

Fulfilled assignment
    requirements   _____

Instructor comments and suggestions:

SafeAssign? Y / N

Time: _____

Score: _____ /100

Listener _____

Speaker _____

Topic _____

Unit 2

INFORMATIVE SPEECH ORGANIZATION

Front page: Complete during the speech.

Briefly outline the speaker's main points below:

I. Introduction

  A. Attention-Getter:

  B. Credibility:

  C. Audience Adaptation:

  D. Thesis/Preview:

II. Body

III. Conclusion

  A. Review:

  B. "When to Clap" Line:

Back page: Complete after the speech is done.

Reflect on how the speaker's organization affected her/his credibility by responding to the following questions:

What organizational pattern did the speaker use in this speech?

What aspects of the speaker's organization improved his/her credibility?

What aspects of the speaker's organization detracted from her/his credibility?

Listener _____ 33

Speaker _____

Topic _____

Unit 2

INFORMATIVE SPEECH RESEARCH

During the speech, record the speaker's source citations and types of supporting material. Then, reflect on the quality of the research as it related to the speaker's credibility and audience adaptation.

Front page: Complete during the speech.

Sources:

Citation	Type of Research
Example	
Point 1:	
Dr. Jones (scientist)	*Book*
Association of Artificial Life Technology	*Web Site*

LISTENING SHEET

Back page: Complete after the speech is done.

Did the speaker cite sources clearly throughout the speech?

Which main points were particularly well-supported with research?

Which main points would have benefited from more support?

Which source citation(s) contributed most to the speaker's credibility? Why?

Which source citation(s) helped the speaker adapt to her/his class audience? Why?

What could the speaker have done differently with his/her sources to improve speaker credibility and audience adaptation?

Listener _____

Speaker _____

Topic _____

Unit 2

INFORMATIVE SPEECH DELIVERY

Identify two of the speaker's delivery *strengths* (comment on any of the following: volume, pitch, rate, pauses, vocal variety, pronunciation, articulation, dialect, appearance, bodily action, gestures, and eye contact).

Identify two areas for improvement in the speaker's delivery (comment on any of the following: volume, pitch, rate, pauses, vocal variety, pronunciation, articulation, dialect, appearance, bodily action, gestures, and eye contact).

What speech preparation or practice techniques would you recommend to the speaker to improve her/his delivery?

LISTENING SHEET

Listener _____

Speaker _____

Topic _____

Unit 2

INFORMATIVE SPEECH VISUAL AID DESIGN

Evaluate the quality of the speaker's visual aid *design*. Were the VAs aesthetically appealing? Why or why not?

In what ways did VA design enhance or detract from the clarity of the message?

Were the VAs in this speech suitable for a professional context? If not, what would you suggest the speaker do differently?

LISTENING SHEET

Listener _____

Speaker _____

Topic _____

Unit 2

INFORMATIVE SPEECH VISUAL AID USE

Comment on how well the speaker *used* visual aids within his/her speech. Did the speaker work with VAs smoothly and confidently?

Evaluate the speaker's eye contact and bodily action as s/he worked with VAs.

How well did the speaker work with VA props and/or technology? (VA stand, overhead projector, computer, etc.)

LISTENING SHEET

Name _____

Topic _____

Unit 2

INFORMATIVE SPEECH

1. What do you feel were the major strengths of the *content* of your speech? (comment on organization, connectives, source citation, and visual aid)

2. What do you feel were the major weaknesses of the *content* of your speech?

3. What do you feel were the best aspects of your speech's *delivery*? (comment on volume, pitch, rate, pauses, vocal variety, pronunciation, articulation, dialect, kinesics, appearance, bodily action, gestures, and eye contact)

SELF-EVALUATION SHEET

4. What aspects of your speech's *delivery* would you like to improve?

5. What elements of this speech do you feel were improved from your last speech?

6. Give an example of how/where/when you might give an informative speech in your future.

7. Has your level of nervousness changed since your last speech? Why or why not?

UNIT 3

INVITATIONAL SPEAKING

Reading: *Invitation to Public Speaking*, Ch. 9, 13, Appendix pages 323–326

Unit Objectives: Upon completion of this unit, you should understand:

- how to enter into a dialogue with your audience in order to explore a complex issue

- how to appreciate multiple perspectives

- how to create a communication environment that allows your audience to participate in a meaningful and productive way

- how your language choices influence the audience members' responses to your message

Assignment: Invitational Dialogue

You will prepare a 5–7 minute speech to explore an issue and then moderate a 3–4 minute dialogue with your class colleagues (maximum of *12 minutes total* for the speech and dialogue). Then you will present a brief conclusion (no more than one minute) summarizing your speech content and dialogue. Your topic should be potentially suitable for the policy speech assignment, and you should use the invitational dialogue as an opportunity to 1) find a topic for your policy speech, and/or 2) gain a greater understanding of and appreciation for your audience's diverse perspectives before you design your policy speech. Cite at least **5–7 different** *sources* for your audience during the speech (put the names of your sources in parentheses when you cite them within the body of your outline). On the day of your dialogues, turn in one copy of a *typed outline* of your invitational speech with *dialogue question prompts* listed at the end and a works cited page. Upload that identical file (with your name removed) to SafeAssign. *Students who do not submit to SafeAssign may receive a zero on their speech.* Avoid spelling, typographical, or grammatical errors.

The Invitational Dialogue Assignment Emphasizes the Following Skills:

- **Organization:** A dialogue can be organized to facilitate clear and comprehensive exploration of an issue.

- **Dialogue:** Before you can ethically and effectively persuade an audience, you must appreciate the multiple sides to every issue and value your audience members' unique perspectives.

- **Speaker Credibility:** In order for audience members to value your opinion, they must feel that you respect them. You can demonstrate this by creating conditions of equality, value, and self-determination.

- **Language:** Your specific word choices can create or inhibit feelings of equality, value, and self-determination.

- **Audience Adaptation:** When audience members feel that you respect them as equals, you value their views, and you will allow them to determine their own courses of action, they are more likely to participate in communicative exchanges in an authentic and meaningful way.

Why It Is Important: Appreciating Multiple Perspectives

The skills you will learn in the invitational speaking unit will serve you well in a variety of professional and personal contexts. Consider the following scenarios:

- You and your parents never discuss politics because you're both so far apart on the issues you just end up having the same fight over and over. One day, you begin a conversation by asking your dad to tell you about the time he was passed over for a promotion and a female colleague got it instead. After he finishes his story, you tell him about an experience a friend of yours had when she was sexually harassed on the job. You both leave the conversation with a broader understanding of a complex social issue. Although neither one of you has changed your mind, the mutual respect you gained by listening to one another will allow you to continue the dialogue in the future.

- You and your partner are having a familiar argument about who should be in charge of various chores at home. Instead of trying to convince your partner that you are right, you ask him/her to explain what's going on in his/her life that makes it difficult to find the time to pitch in around the house. Feeling validated by your genuine concern, your partner asks you the same question. The conversation allows both of you to frame the problem differently. Rather than asking the question, "how can we split housework equally?" you both ask the question, "how can we work together to achieve our goals both inside and outside the home? How can we maximize each other's skills and minimize each other's frustrations?"

- You have been promoted to a management position at work. Your predecessor was let go because of his inability to get the staff to work together and maintain high productivity. In your first staff meeting, you conduct a dialogue with your staff using the principles of equality, value, and self-determination. The staff provides you with valuable insight about their specific jobs, knowledge that you never could obtain without performing each job personally. In addition, because you began your meeting by asking for their input, your staff feels more invested in the organization. Open lines of communication foster respect and loyalty, which in turn helps the staff function more effectively.

- You are a member of your local school board. The board is being asked to consider a new science curriculum. Aspects of the curriculum, such as the origins of the universe and the nature of human life, are controversial. You do not have special training in science or philosophy but you want to make a decision that serves the community in a fair and responsible way. Before the board votes, you convene a hearing in which members of the community with special insight into science, philosophy, religion, and education are invited to share their perspective on the appropriateness of the proposed curriculum. Not only do you broaden your knowledge base before voting on the new curriculum, you also give opponents and supporters of the measure an equal opportunity to be heard. If the vote does not go their way, they at least will know that members of their community value their perspective and include them in discussions.

Sample Invitational Speech Outline
for Analysis and Discussion

SPCM 200, [Section]
[Date]

Organic Farming vs. Conventional Farming

by Anthony Scholl[1]

Specific Purpose Statement: To invite my audience to consider the advantages and disadvantages associated with organic and conventional farming practices and to explore the future of farming.

Thesis: Organic farming is a special farming technique that differs greatly from conventional farming and is becoming very popular today; today, I would like to understand these differences in order to make a more informed choice on my own food purchasing behavior.

Introduction

I. [*Attention-Getter*] Imagine you are walking through the fresh produce section of a grocery store and with every type of fruit or vegetable there are two different options to buy.

    A. You are there to buy fresh red apples.

    B. You see two different bins containing these red apples and you look to distinguish the difference.

    C. One bin has the label "Organic" on it while the other simply says "Red Apples."

    D. What is the difference between these apples? Why don't they both cost the same?

II. [*Reveal topic and relate to audience*] With organic farming becoming more popular, we face the decision to purchase organic or conventional foods so we need to be knowledgeable about both types of food.

III. [*Establish credibility*] I have been working for a company called L&J Farms for four years and I have had experience with both organic and conventional farming techniques.

    A. I have never really taken the time to research the exact differences between the two techniques until this speech.

    B. After researching the advantages and disadvantages to organic and conventional farming techniques, I am still undecided which to purchase for my own consumption.

IV. [*Thesis and Preview*] Therefore, I would first like to present you the definition of organic farming and then **explore** the differences between organic farming and conventional farming.

    A. I hope by sharing this information today and then hearing your opinions on the topic, I will be able to decide which type of produce I should purchase.

---

1 The original outline has been updated and modified by the Basic Course Director to reflect the evolving expectations of the public speaking course.

B. I also hope at the end of our discussion today that you will be able to make a more informed decision on your food purchasing behaviors.

Signpost: First, we will look at organic farming.

Body

I. According to an article titled "Organic Farming – Definition," organic farming is the process of producing food naturally.

  A. This method avoids the use of synthetic chemical fertilizers and genetically modified organisms to influence the growth of crops.

  B. These foods are grown on land that has been absent of any chemicals for a minimum of 3 years. Therefore, consuming organic food reduces the risk of introducing foreign chemicals or residues into your body.

  C. According to the article "Perceived Pros and Cons of Organic Food," organic farming is good for the environment.

    1. Organic farming techniques allow farmers to use less energy and produce less waste.

    2. Because synthetic pesticides are not used in organic farming, things such as chemical runoff do not harm local wildlife.

    3. Organic farming helps sustain natural ecosystems by a strategy called crop rotation.

  D. According to an article titled "Organic Food Basics," organic food advocates claim that organically grown foods are more nutritious and safer than conventionally grown foods.

    1. However, studies investigating whether organic foods are in fact higher in nutritional value show mixed results.

    2. They may have slightly higher nutritional content but not enough to make it conclusive.

  E. On the contrary, organic farming does have a few disadvantages.

    1. First, because organic farming does not include the use of chemicals or genetically modified organisms, organic foods are not prevented from disease.

    2. Another downside to organic food is that on average, consumers pay 50 percent more for organic products and up to 100 percent more for organic meat and dairy products ("Perceived Pros and Cons of Organic Food").

  F. Personally, I believe that organic farming is an important practice to help sustain our ecosystem. However, I also have some concerns over the cost of production for organic farmers, as well as the current cost to consumers.

Transition: Now that we have a background of organic farming, let's take a look at the conventional farming method.

II. According to the website CoExtra.eu, conventional farming is farming where chemical plant protectants, chemical fertilizers, and intensive mass animal farming are common.

A. This farming method has dominated the 20th century and it is also the most common method today (CoExtra.eu).

B. By incorporating growth hormones in animals or pesticides and fertilizers in crops, farmers are able to mass produce commodities to meet the market's demands.

C. With a rapidly growing population in the United States, it is important for farmers to produce enough food to keep up with the population growth.

D. Conventional farming is also less expensive than organic farming due to fewer restrictions and less labor required.

E. Conventional food has a good price market and as long as people continue to buy this food, this market will thrive.

    1. According to (Dairy Farming Today), "less than 2 percent of the U.S. population is involved in farming today" yet the population continues to grow.

    2. Personally, I worry what would happen to our food supply if conventional farming practices cease to exist.

F. Also, like I said before, the chemicals and genetically modified organisms used in conventional farming help prevent disease.

G. With this being said, conventional farming also has its downsides.

    1. Scientists have noted that this farming technique has very harmful effects on the environment and surrounding ecosystems. ("What REALLY Makes Our Food Grow?")

    2. Chemical runoff has very damaging effects to the environment and the animals that live nearby.

    3. The main issue with conventional farming is the degradation of soil.

        a. Farmers are finding out today that they are at a lack of nutrient rich soil.

        b. Not only does this harm their food production but it also leaves a very small chance that the soil is able to support an ecosystem.

Now that I have shared with you some of the advantages and disadvantages to organic and conventional farming, I'd like to hear your thoughts and opinions on the topic.

Dialogue Questions

I. Close-Ended Questions

    A. By a show of hands, how many of you purchase food based on the way it is produced?

    B. By a show of hands, how many of you choose to purchase organic products? Why?

II. Open-Ended Questions

    A. Are there reasons for choosing organic products that I did not discuss in my speech today? If so, what are they?

B. On a scale of 1 to 5 (5 = always; 1 = never), how often do you purchase organic products?

C. For those of you who do not choose organic products, why not?

D. I mentioned in my speech that less than 2 percent of the U.S. population is involved in farming. What do you think this means for our future food supply?

E. In what way(s) might this influence organic farming? Conventional farming?

Conclusion

I. [*Signal End*] As we have learned today,

II. [*Review*] Organic farming is a special farming technique that differs greatly from conventional farming and is becoming very popular today.

    A. We have explored the advantages and disadvantages of the two farming techniques to further our understanding about the food products that we as consumers are purchasing.

    B. Using what we have learned today, I hope we are now able to make our own personal decisions on whether to buy organic food or conventional food based on our own preferences.

III. [*Closing Line*] I encourage you all to think back to the information presented in this speech the next time you are at the grocery store standing in front of two different apple bins.

Works Cited

"Conventional Farming." *Co-Extra.* 2006. Web. 18 Oct. 2009.

"Dairy Farming Today." n.d. Web. 15 Jan. 2010.

Fong, Bethany. "Organic Foods." *Food and Culture*, n.d. Web.18 Oct. 2009.

"Harm From Conventional Farming." *Om Organics.* 2004. Web. 18 Oct. 2009.

Jegtvig, Shereen. "Organic Food Basics." About.com. 2008. Web. 18 Oct. 2009.

"Organic: Lower Carbon, Less Energy, All Natural." *Farmers Weekly.* 2008. Web. 18 Oct. 2009.

Roth, Rebecca. "Organic or Not Organic?" 9 Jan. 2008. Web. 18 Oct. 2009.

"What REALLY Makes Our Food Grow?" n.d. Web. 18 Oct. 2009.

UNIT 3 INVITATIONAL SPEAKING

Name_____

Date_____

Unit 3

INVITATIONAL DIALOGUE

Propose two potential topics for your Invitational Dialogue. List them below, in order of preference.

Topic 1:

Thesis statement:

What other perspectives on this topic are necessary to consider as you organize your speech?

If this topic is approved, what kind of questions might you ask as part of your facilitation? Be sure to include examples of both open-ended and close-ended questions.

TOPIC PROPOSAL

Topic 2:

Thesis statement:

What other perspectives on this topic are necessary to consider as you organize your speech?

If this topic is approved, what kind of questions might you ask as part of your facilitation? Be sure to include examples of both open-ended and closed-ended questions.

Instructor Comments:

Topic 1 __ Approved __ Not Approved

Topic 2 __ Approved __ Not Approved

Speaker _____   53

Listener _____

Topic _____

Unit 3

INVITATIONAL DIALOGUE

In what ways, if at all, did this speaker create an invitational speaking environment (conditions of equality, value, and self-determination)?

List examples of invitational language you heard in this person's speech. If there were none, identify language choices that may have inhibited the invitational environment.

Can you suggest strategies the speaker could have used to enhance the invitational environment during their speech and dialogue?

What question(s) or concern(s) did you have about the speaker's topic after hearing the speech?

FEEDBACK

Speaker _____   55

Listener _____

Topic _____

Unit 3

INVITATIONAL DIALOGUE

In what ways, if at all, did this speaker create an invitational speaking environment (conditions of equality, value, and self-determination)?

List examples of invitational language you heard in this person's speech. If there were none, identify language choices that may have inhibited the invitational environment.

Can you suggest strategies the speaker could have used to enhance the invitational environment during their speech and dialogue?

What question(s) or concern(s) did you have about the speaker's topic after hearing the speech?

FEEDBACK

Speaker _____

Listener _____

Topic _____

Unit 3

INVITATIONAL DIALOGUE

In what ways, if at all, did this speaker create an invitational speaking environment (conditions of equality, value, and self-determination)?

List examples of invitational language you heard in this person's speech. If there were none, identify language choices that may have inhibited the invitational environment.

Can you suggest strategies the speaker could have used to enhance the invitational environment during their speech and dialogue?

What question(s) or concern(s) did you have about the speaker's topic after hearing the speech?

FEEDBACK

UNIT 3 INVITATIONAL SPEAKING

Speaker _____

Listener _____

Topic _____

Unit 3

INVITATIONAL DIALOGUE

In what ways, if at all, did this speaker create an invitational speaking environment (conditions of equality, value, and self-determination)?

List examples of invitational language you heard in this person's speech. If there were none, identify language choices that may have inhibited the invitational environment.

Can you suggest strategies the speaker could have used to enhance the invitational environment during their speech and dialogue?

What question(s) or concern(s) did you have about the speaker's topic after hearing the speech?

FEEDBACK

UNIT 3 INVITATIONAL SPEAKING

Speaker _____

Topic _____

Unit 3

INVITATIONAL DIALOGUE

+ Excellent   **✓ Satisfactory**   **-- Needs improvement**   **0 Failed to complete**

INTRODUCTION
Gained audience attention _____
Established credibility _____
Introduced topic in an
   invitational way _____
Related topic to audience _____
Clear thesis/preview _____

BODY: ORGANIZATION
Main points were clear _____
Presented topic fairly _____
Effective connectives _____
Incorporated invitational language _____

BODY: RESEARCH
Main points fully supported _____
Adequate variety of sources _____
Used credible sources _____
Cited sources orally _____

DIALOGUE
Smooth transition to dialogue _____
Appropriate question prompts _____
Facilitated effectively _____
Invitational environment: _____
   Equality _____
   Value _____
   Self-Determination _____
Allowed multiple people
   to participate _____

CONCLUSION
Signaled end of speech _____
Ended with artistic last line _____

Specific strengths and areas for improvement:

CRITIQUE SHEET

DELIVERY

Maintained eye contact _____
Used vocal variety _____
Projected adequately _____
Pronunciation correct _____
Articulation clear _____
Rate appropriate _____
Paused effectively _____
Gestures purposeful _____
Proxemics effective _____
Mannerisms appropriate _____
Facial expression _____
Spoke fluently _____
Extemporaneous style _____
Effective use of speaking notes _____

OUTLINE

Complete sentence format _____
Logical subordination _____
Labels included _____
Works Cited page _____
Accurate spelling _____
Correct grammar _____
Free of typos/errors _____
Include appropriate
   discussion questions _____

ADDITIONAL ITEMS

Topic appropriate _____
Completed in time limit _____
Fulfilled assignment
   requirements _____

Instructor comments and suggestions:

SafeAssign? Y / N

Speech Time: _____

Dialogue Time: _____

Total Time: _____

Score: _____ /200

Speaker _____

Topic _____

Unit 3

INVITATIONAL DIALOGUE

+ Excellent   **✓ Satisfactory**   **-- Needs improvement**   **0 Failed to complete**

INTRODUCTION

Specific strengths and areas for improvement:

Gained audience attention   _____

Established credibility   _____

Introduced topic in an
   invitational way   _____

Related topic to audience   _____

Clear thesis/preview   _____

BODY: ORGANIZATION

Main points were clear   _____

Presented topic fairly   _____

Effective connectives   _____

Incorporated invitational language   _____

BODY: RESEARCH

Main points fully supported   _____

Adequate variety of sources   _____

Used credible sources   _____

Cited sources orally   _____

DIALOGUE

Smooth transition to dialogue   _____

Appropriate question prompts   _____

Facilitated effectively   _____

Invitational environment: _____
   Equality   _____
   Value   _____
   Self-Determination   _____

Allowed multiple people
   to participate   _____

CONCLUSION

Signaled end of speech   _____

Ended with artistic last line   _____

CRITIQUE SHEET

DELIVERY

Maintained eye contact   _____

Used vocal variety   _____

Projected adequately   _____

Pronunciation correct   _____

Articulation clear   _____

Rate appropriate   _____

Paused effectively   _____

Gestures purposeful   _____

Proxemics effective   _____

Mannerisms appropriate   _____

Facial expression   _____

Spoke fluently   _____

Extemporaneous style   _____

Effective use of speaking notes   _____

OUTLINE

Complete sentence format   _____

Logical subordination   _____

Labels included   _____

Works Cited page   _____

Accurate spelling   _____

Correct grammar   _____

Free of typos/errors   _____

Include appropriate
  discussion questions   _____

ADDITIONAL ITEMS

Topic appropriate   _____

Completed in time limit   _____

Fulfilled assignment
  requirements   _____

Instructor comments and suggestions:

SafeAssign? Y / N

Speech Time: _____

Dialogue Time: _____

Total Time: _____

Score: _____ **/200**

Name _____

Topic _____

Unit 3

INVITATIONAL DIALOGUE

1. What was the most challenging component of this speech for you? Why? How did you respond to that challenge in your speech?

2. How did audience participation make this speech different from the last speech for you as a speaker? Was the experience better or worse than your last speech? Why?

3. What do you feel were the best aspects of your speech's *delivery*? (comment on volume, pitch, rate, pauses, vocal variety, pronunciation, articulation, dialect, kinesics, appearance, bodily action, gestures, and eye contact)

SELF-EVALUATION SHEET

4. What aspects of your speech's *delivery* would you like to improve?

5. What elements of this speech do you feel were improved from your last speech?

6. Give an example of how/where/when you might use an invitational speech in your future.

7. Has your level of nervousness changed since your last speech? Why or why not?

UNIT 4
PERSUASIVE SPEAKING

Reading: *Invitation to Public Speaking*, Ch. 14–15

Unit Objectives: Upon completion of this unit, you should understand:

- how persuasive speaking is different from informative or invitational speaking

- how to adapt to an audience that might be unconcerned about or opposed to your ideas

- how to build an argument with evidence

- effective methods of reasoning

- how to appeal to emotions

- the types of organization for persuasive speeches

Assignment: Policy Speech

Prepare and present a 6–8 minute speech that proposes a plan to solve a current public problem. After your 8 minute speech, field 2–3 minutes worth of questions from the audience. You may arrange your policy speech into the problem-solution organizational pattern, the problem-cause-solution pattern, the comparative advantages organizational pattern, or Monroe's motivated sequence. Make sure to relate your discussion of the problem and proposed solution specifically to your class audience. **It is highly recommended that you do not come up with your own policy, but *find* a policy to advocate or *adopt* for a new context.** Cite at least *6–8 different sources* for your audience during the speech (put the names of your sources in parentheses when you cite them within the body of your outline). Prior to the delivery of the speech, submit one copy of a typed complete-sentence outline, including a works cited page to your instructor. Upload that identical file (with your name removed) to SafeAssign. *Students who do not submit to SafeAssign may receive a zero on their speech.* Avoid spelling, typographical, or grammatical errors.

The Policy Speech Assignment Emphasizes the Following Skills:

- **Organization:** Choose an organizational pattern that suits your topic and persuasive goals.

- **Argument:** Well-developed arguments should support your persuasive claims. Include clear logical appeals, appropriate emotional appeals, and thorough research.

- **Speaker Credibility:** Every aspect of your performance, from topic selection to research to delivery, should evidence your personal credibility as a speaker.

- **Audience Adaptation:** Your speech should show evidence of careful audience analysis and specific audience adaptation. Anticipate and respond to potential counterarguments against your proposed plan.

- **Visual Support:** Visual aids are optional this time, but strongly suggested. Visual support can help illustrate and support your persuasive claims.

Why It Is Important: Learning to Advocate for Change

Part of being a responsible citizen is being prepared to advocate for change when change is needed. Many people would prefer to be "armchair quarterbacks" when it comes to solving problems in their home, school, workplace, or community. It is easy to debunk other people's proposals for change. It's tougher to come up with a constructive, workable solution to a problem. The policy speech assignment is designed to teach skills vital to democratic citizenship: identifying a problem that affects other people, coming up with a workable and beneficial plan for change, and convincing others that they should support your course of action.

Skills learned from the policy speech are not just relevant for the "politically minded." There are many times in our lives when the ability to argue for a specific policy could benefit us personally. Negotiating for flex time at work, participating in a homeowner's association or athletic league board, advocating that your local gym change its class schedule—each of these scenarios involves the advocacy skills on which we focus in this unit. When you become a credible advocate for change, you empower yourself, benefit others, and experience the positive changes that occur as a result of your efforts.

Tips and Suggestions: The Argument Triangle

©Hayden-McNeil, LLC

The argument triangle provides a simple but concrete way to visualize how you should develop arguments in your policy speech. Every argument has three components: 1) a clear persuasive claim, 2) evidence from your research that supports and illustrates the claim, and 3) your own analysis that connects the evidence to the claim. Evaluate each main point in your speech. Everyone should begin with a clear claim that is supported with evidence that directly proves your claim. Round out each main point with your own analysis.

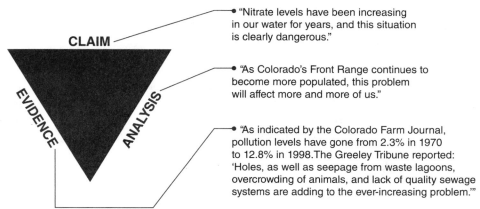

CLAIM

EVIDENCE

ANALYSIS

- "Nitrate levels have been increasing in our water for years, and this situation is clearly dangerous."

- "As Colorado's Front Range continues to become more populated, this problem will affect more and more of us."

- "As indicated by the Colorado Farm Journal, pollution levels have gone from 2.3% in 1970 to 12.8% in 1998.The Greeley Tribune reported: 'Holes, as well as seepage from waste lagoons, overcrowding of animals, and lack of quality sewage systems are adding to the ever-increasing problem.'"

©Hayden-McNeil, LLC

Advocating for a Policy: Need, Plan, and Practicality

by AnnaMarie Adams Mann

The first step in understanding questions of policy is to know which *issues* you, as a speaker, must address when advocating for a specific policy change. There are three issues that must be addressed: **NEED**, **PLAN**, and **PRACTICALITY**.

NEED: Before presenting a policy or plan of action, you must demonstrate that a current problem exists and that it relates to your specific audience. To support this claim, you must use credible evidence (i.e., examples, statistics, narratives, definitions, and/or testimonies) that illustrates the severity of the problem and, simultaneously, connects the problem to the audience. Information relevant to the need argument includes (but may not be limited to) the following:

- A general explanation of the problem

- The population that is affected by the problem

- The severity of the problem

- The dangers involved if the problem is not fixed

PLAN: Now that you have persuaded your audience that there is a "need" for change, the next step is to present a plan that responds to this "need." An effective plan not only solves the problem, but also addresses questions such as: Who will implement the plan? Who will enforce the plan? Who will fund the plan? Although the presentation of a plan will vary by context, the format below may provide a good starting point:

- *Explain your plan:* What does your plan entail? What are the specific courses of action you advocate implementing?

- *State who will enforce the plan:* For example, if regulating the nutritional value of fast food, would you rely on the industry to police itself or would you require the FDA (Food and Drug Administration) to enforce it?

- *Discuss funding:* Remember—funding doesn't have to always come from taxes. Sometimes the money needed to support a policy comes from reallocating existing funds.

PRACTICALITY: When presenting a plan, a speaker must also demonstrate that the plan is practical and, thus, the best solution to employ. To show the practicality of a plan, you will need to address three areas:

- *Cure:* Does the "plan" solve the problems presented in the "need" section of your speech? You can support this claim by providing examples of your plan successfully implemented in other contexts, citing expert testimony that suggests your plan is a recommended course of action, drawing analogies that illustrate why your plan is a good response to the problem, and/or providing statistics or other evidence that supports your reasoning.

- *Advantages outweigh disadvantages:* With every plan, disadvantages are going to arise. As the speaker, it is your responsibility to show how the advantages/benefits of the plan outweigh the disadvantages/costs. Remember, costs can be monetary but can also be measured in other ways (such as loss of liberty, ethical costs, etc.).

- *Counterarguments:* When persuading an audience, counterarguments are bound to arise. In order to stop those counterarguments from snowballing and interfering with your persuasive appeal, you can address them in your speech and follow with a statement that contests that argument.

Fitting Need, Plan, and Practicality into an Organizational Pattern

Now that you understand the three issues that need to be addressed when advocating for a policy, you need to know how this information relates to the organizational patterns used to write a policy speech. Four examples are provided below:

PROBLEM-SOLUTION

If using a problem-solution pattern, your body will consist of two main points. The first main point should address the problem that you are presenting to your audience. As such, you will develop your "need" arguments in this main point. The second main point should address the solution and, therefore, should include both the "plan" and the "practicality" of your plan.

> **BODY**
>
> I. **Problem (includes need)**
>
> II. **Solution (includes plan and practicality)**

PROBLEM-CAUSE-SOLUTION

If using a problem-cause-solution pattern, your body will consist of three main points. The first main point should address the problem that you are presenting to your audience. As such, you will include your evidence supporting the "need" in this main point. The second main point should detail the cause of the problem. Similar to the first main point, the cause will be supported with evidence you gathered to support the "need" for a plan. The third main point addresses the solution and, therefore, should include both the "plan" and the "practicality" of your plan.

BODY

  I.   **Problem (includes need)**

  II. **Cause (includes need)**

  III. **Solution (includes plan and practicality)**

COMPARATIVE ADVANTAGE

If using the comparative advantage pattern, your body will consist of three main points. The first main point should address the current policy in use to address the problem you are concerned with. Therefore, you should describe "need" in point one, particularly identifying what the need is. The second point should outline why the current approach to the problem is insufficient. In other words, "need" is also described here because you want to tell the audience why the problem persists despite a policy that tries to fix it. The third main point addresses what your alternative policy would be and argues why it will be more effective than the existing policy. As such, include your plan and practicality here. Remember to end with a compelling conclusion.

BODY

  I.   **Current Policy (includes need)**

  II. **Deficiencies of Current Policy (includes need)**

  III. **New Policy and Why It's Better (includes plan and practicality)**

MONROE'S MOTIVATED SEQUENCE

If using Monroe's Motivated Sequence, your body will consist of five points (two of which will replace the introduction and conclusion). The first point should quickly and effectively garner your audience's attention. The second point should address the problem that you are presenting to your audience. As such, you will include your evidence supporting the "need" in this main point. The third main point addresses the solution and, therefore, should include both the "plan" and the "practicality" of your plan. The fourth main point—Visualization—can reinforce the effects of your solution in either a positive or negative way. Your fifth point will feature your call to action.

BODY

  I.   **Attention**

  II. **Need (includes need)**

  III. **Solution (includes plan and practicality)**

  IV. **Visualization**

  V.   **Action**

Fielding Questions After a Persuasive Speech

There are many situations that require the ability to field questions in a calm and convincing manner—job interviews, training sessions, professional presentations, and interpersonal debates. The purpose of Q&A in this class is to familiarize you with strategies for fielding questions successfully, and to expose you to an actual Q&A session.

OBJECTIVES OF THE Q&A SESSION

- Clarify information

- Expand or reinforce your arguments

- Bolster your credibility

- Assuage listener concerns

Q&A FRAME OF MIND

Competence

A question session should showcase your communication competence. Reinforce your claims for the audience and be prepared to explain and extend your arguments with new examples and additional evidence. There is usually information that you cannot include in your speech due to time constraints—this is your opportunity to share that information with the audience.

Never fake it—audiences can spot a phony a mile away. Be willing to admit areas of ignorance by saying something like, "That's an aspect of the topic I haven't considered in depth," or "That's a good suggestion. I would like to pursue that in further research."

Collaboration

A question session is not a confrontation. You want to win over your audience, not beat them in an argument. Even though some audience members might bait you and try to engage you in confrontation, do not risk it. You will end up undermining your own credibility if you go "one-on-one" with a listener. Instead, emphasize areas of convergence between your arguments and the questioner's position. Listen carefully to the questions that are posed. Be willing to admit areas of ignorance or weaknesses in your argument. Remember, the effectiveness of a speech is judged by how well it is adjusted to the audience.

Control

When you are the speaker, you get to control the presentation. If you need a moment or two to think about a question before you respond, take it! Do not relinquish control of your topic by "buying into" someone else's premise. Do not allow one questioner to dominate the Q&A session—acknowledge others after you have given one audience member the opportunity for a question and follow-up question/response.

Common Sense

Do not feel that everyone is "out to get you" after you have given a speech. People have different motivations for asking questions—to seek clarification, to make themselves look smart, to help you support your claims, or to contradict you. Not all questions are hostile. That is why listening is an especially important skill during a Q&A session.

Q&A STRATEGIES
Answer Format

1. Listen for the concept and assess the questioner's motivation.

2. Restate the question aloud if it needs clarification or if you want to make sure you are interpreting it correctly.

3. State your answer succinctly.

4. Support your answer → reiterate what you said in your speech or offer new information or evidence.

Nonverbal Behavior

- As you answer a question, look at the questioner first, but scan the whole audience.

- Maintain a firm, authoritative stance. Try to minimize distracting gestures and movements.

- Try to look and feel relaxed.

Responding to specific types of questions:

- *Loaded questions:* "Don't you know that environmental regulation costs jobs?" Acknowledge the listener's position/emotions. State your position without buying into the listener's premise. Try to emphasize areas of convergence between the two positions.

  - Ex: "It sounds like you're concerned about the economic implications of my proposal. That's understandable since previous regulations have had a negative effect on local economies. In fact, that was one of my main concerns as I was researching and developing this plan. However, by training businesses to use the environment more efficiently, I'm ensuring that the resources they need to keep their businesses going will be in plentiful supply for years to come. Without some sort of change in how businesses interact with the environment, local companies will have to shut down or move operations out of this region in just ten to twenty years."

- *Complex questions:* "I wonder which regulatory measures are best, most effective, and how much each costs?"

  - State that the question has several parts, and you will answer it piece by piece. Do not feel compelled to answer every issue. Feel free to focus on the most important/relevant question(s).

- Vague questions: "What do you think about NAFTA?"

  - Clarify with the questioner what s/he is trying to find out about before you attempt to answer.

- Statement of open disagreement/hostility: "I can't believe you cited something from PETA—they are the most radical animal rights group around. They care more about animals than people!"

  - Tell the listener you understand how s/he feels, answer the specific objection, find areas of convergence if possible, then move on to another question. Never allow hostility to escalate.

Sample Policy Speech Outline
for Analysis and Discussion

SPCM 200, [Section]
[Date]

The Education Gap

by Maaike Godfrey[1]

Specific Purpose Statement: To persuade my audience that there is inequality in our nation's schools, and propose a policy change to rectify the situation.

Thesis: Our nation's schools provide drastically different levels of education to children depending on their family's income status, and while there is no simple solution, there are first steps that need to be taken to ultimately resolve this problem.

Pattern of Organization: Problem/Cause/Solution

Introduction

I. [*Attention-Getter*] In London, the underground train system is called the tube.

    A. According to the travel article ("Getting Around London" from TravelLondon.com), at each tube station, the public is warned about the space between the platform and the train.

        1. Signs reading "Mind the Gap" are prominently displayed.

        2. An announcer with a strong British accent also repeats the phrase over the loud speaker.

    B. Well, I think it's time for the United States to adopt the slogan, but in a very different context.

II. [*Reveal topic and relate to audience*] Our educational system is set up in such a way that funding varies drastically from district to district.

    A. Schools consistently spend less per student in low-income districts than high-income districts.

    B. As a result, there is an ever-widening achievement gap between most of America's youth and those from lower socio-economic statuses.

III. [*Establish credibility*] For the past semester I have been volunteering at Creative Options Education Center, a private, non-profit that attempts to address that gap by serving young at-risk youth before they get into the public school system.

    A. I also feel a personal connection to this issue, as I am the product of a low-income family and will be the first person in my immediate family to obtain a college degree.

    B. I have done additional research on this topic as well, so I feel very qualified to talk to you about it today.

---

1 The original outline has been updated and modified by the Basic Course Director to reflect the evolving expectations of the public speaking course.

IV. [*Thesis and Preview*] As I said before, our nation's schools provide drastically different levels of education to children depending on their family's income status, and while there is no simple solution, there are first steps that need to be taken to ultimately resolve this problem.

   A. The level of education our youth receive directly impacts many of the problems facing the nation and our country's place in the global market.

   B. While the issue is a national one, I will lay out a plan that addresses the problems initially on a state level.

   C. The impacts of improving our education system will be felt not just by the students receiving the education they deserve, but by the whole country.

[Signpost] I will now go into the most important aspects of this convoluted issue and present a plan for instigating the much-needed change.

Body

I. [*Problem/Need*] The hard data about our public education system, kept by the (U.S. Department of Education) and numerous non-profit organizations, clearly shows the disparities in funding that our schools receive.

   A. According to the report *Funding Gap 2007*, published by the non-profit non-partisan organization (The Education Trust), low-income school districts, on average, receive $938 less per student per year than their high-income counterparts.

      1. That number might not sound extraordinarily high, but when you consider that a school in a low-income district serving 500 students will receive almost $500,000 less per year than a school in a high-income district, the number is staggering.

      2. But when you look beyond the national average, that number jumps to $1.5 million per year for a school serving 500 children, according to the (New York State School Board Association's "Legislative Summary" for 2007).

   B. Why does this matter?

      1. Well, we all know—after listening to speeches in this class—there are a lot more problems created by lack of education than we may realize, including:

         a. homelessness

         b. hunger

         c. poverty

         d. the lack of accessible healthcare

      2. All of these issues could be drastically reduced by providing a good education to each and every child.

         a. This solution would attend to **immediate** problems facing those not fortunate enough to be born into a middle- or upper-class family.

    b. Data from *Funding Gap 2007* also shows that children who do not receive an adequate education have a much higher chance than their well-educated peers of needing public assistance **later in life**.

[Transition] So what is causing this disparity?

II. [*Cause/Need*] Our public schools are funded in large part on the local level, by property taxes levied on homeowners in each school district. This is according to the online report, (*Level Playing Field? The Implications of School Funding*, published by the CfBT Education Trust).

    A. Property taxes greatly influence the funding disparity between schools.

        1. In wealthy areas where homes are worth more, more property taxes are generated and more money goes to the public schools in that area.

        2. In districts that have high poverty rates, property values are lower, tax revenues are lower, and the public schools therefore receive less money.

    B. The system ultimately perpetuates poverty.

        1. According to the *Condition of Education* 2003 report, published online by the (U.S. Department of Education), 80% of high-income students go to college after high school.

        2. The same report states just 44% of their low-income peers do the same.

[Transition] I recognize that this is a very grave issue, and if the solution were simple it would already be in place. But I also believe that there are steps we can take to turn things around.

III. [*Solution/Plan*] The plan that I propose would occur on a state level, with oversight from the federal government.

    A. The reason for this is that while the problem is a national one, the educational system is set up in a way that places most educational responsibilities and oversight in the hands of the state, and I believe that is where the problems can be rectified.

    B. I propose that the funding of schools be changed from a localized system to a centralized system. It would have three primary features:

        1. A state would collect the percentage of property taxes that go to education in one general account.

        2. It would then add to that the federal funds that have been allotted.

        3. The monies would then be distributed to the school districts on a per student basis.

    C. The change would need to be mandated by the federal government, but then it would be up to the individual states to rewrite their existing legislation.

    D. Because this plan calls for a reallocation of funds there would be no tax increases involved.

    E. Though it would be ideal for this change to be brought about immediately, realistically it would take years for the states to establish a new system.

[Transition] Now that I've described my plan to solve the problem of the funding gap in public schools, I'd like to tell you why this plan will work.

IV. *[Solution/Practicality]*

    A. My plan would ensure that every child is given an equitable education, and therefore a chance to reach their full potential.

        1. Tax sharing plans like the one I am proposing have been used in other cities and states.

            a. For example, Minneapolis and St. Paul, Minnesota put such a system in place in 1975.

            b. Michigan and Connecticut have also both explored these options.

        2. Where previous efforts have been fully undertaken, they have been moderately successful in lessening the gap between rich and poor.

            a. According to the "Regional Tax-Base or Revenue Sharing" published on the Commercial Real Estate Development Association's website, in Minneapolis and St. Paul, Minnesota, "[tax sharing] has notably reduced disparities among the localities included in the pool concerning their assessed non-residential property values per capita."

            b. In Minnesota, where the greatest disparity in 1975 was 50 to 1, by 2007 it was 12 to 1 ("Regional Tax-Base or Revenue Sharing").

    B. *[Counterarguments]* The major counterargument to my plan comes from those families in high-income communities, who would see a drop in funds that their children's schools receive.

        1. While this plan does call for that to happen, I challenge those people to look at the long-term advantages.

            a. They are already paying to support low-income members of society in the form of Medicaid, food stamps, and welfare programs.

            b. The long-term change would be that instead of paying for those people's welfare checks and food stamps they would be paying for their education.

        2. So the question becomes, would you prefer to pay for a person's education and help them lead a life of self-sufficiency, or would you rather pay for that same person when they need welfare, food stamps, or incarceration?

    C. *[Advantages vs. Disadvantages]* The advantage to educating all of our children to a level that allows them to compete in the global market will be felt by everyone. However, there are a few disadvantages to my plan.

        1. One disadvantage is that people might initially disagree with having the taxes they pay going to help other, more needy school districts.

        2. Another disadvantage was mentioned earlier in my speech, and that is that the rewards from reforming the existing funding structure for schools may not be felt for many years.

    a.   The long-term advantages of having a school system where every child has a chance to become educated far outweigh the disadvantages of the initial anger and impatience people may feel with the plan.

    b.   As more people become qualified for higher-paying jobs, our economy will benefit from an increase in the amount of consumer dollars being spent, the income taxes collected by the federal and state governments will go up, and fewer people will need government assistance to pay for the necessities.

Conclusion

I.   [*Signal End*] The problems facing our nation are numerous. The issue that I have discussed today plays a central role in the solutions for those problems.

II.   [*Review*] As our public education system currently stands, our nation's children are receiving very inequitable educations.

    A.   We need to ensure that every student has the opportunity to achieve his or her highest potential, and we as a society will benefit by doing so.

    B.   I propose that school funding be centralized on a state level so that every child receives what he or she needs to succeed.

    C.   Taxes would not be increased to implement my plan, and many other issues facing our society would be positively impacted by instituting it.

III.   [*Closing Line*] In closing, I ask that as you think about the world that we are inheriting, remember: mind the gap!

[page break between end of speech and Works Cited page]

Works Cited

Arroyo, C. G. *The Funding Gap*. The Education Trust. 2 Sept. 2007. Web. 23 Nov. 2010.

Condition of Education 2003. U.S. Department of Education. 1 June 2003. Web. 23 Nov. 2010.

"Getting Around London." *Travel London.com*. 15 Aug. 2007. Web. 23 Nov. 2010.

"Legislative Summary 2007." *New York State School Boards Association*. 1 June 2007. Web. 23 Nov. 2010.

"Regional Tax-Base or Revenue Sharing." *NAIOP: Commercial Real Estate Development Association*. NAIOP: Commercial Real Estate Development Association, 2010. Web. 18 Nov. 2010.

Sibieta, L., Chowdry, H., and Muriel, A. "Level Playing Field? The Implications of School Funding." CfBT Education Trust. June 2007. Web. 18 Nov. 2010.

UNIT 4 PERSUASIVE SPEAKING

Name_____

Date_____

Unit 4

POLICY SPEECH

Review the policy model requirements for the assignment. Then, identify two potential topics for your policy speech and do preliminary research on both. Make sure that your topics are unique, narrow enough to cover in the time allotted, and adapted to your class audience. List them below in order of preference.

PROBLEM 1:

A. State succinctly the nature of the public problem:

B. List the ways in which this problem causes serious harms to people, property, institutions, nature, etc.

C. What proposal(s) for change do you plan to offer to solve this problem?

List at least three articles you have found on this topic *from this year and last year only*:

1. Author_____ Title _____

    Publication _____ Pages _____ Date _____

2. Author_____ Title _____

    Publication _____ Pages _____ Date _____

3. Author_____ Title _____

    Publication _____ Pages _____ Date _____

TOPIC PROPOSAL

PROBLEM 2:

A. State succinctly the nature of the public problem:

B. List the ways in which this problem causes serious harms to people, property, institutions, nature, etc.

C. What proposal(s) for change do you plan to offer to solve this problem?

List at least three articles you have found on this topic *from this year and last year only*:

1. Author_____ Title _____

    Publication _____ Pages _____ Date _____

2. Author_____ Title _____

    Publication _____ Pages _____ Date _____

3. Author_____ Title _____

    Publication _____ Pages _____ Date _____

Name_____

Topic_____

Date_____

Unit 4

POLICY SPEECH

No matter which organizational pattern you choose for your policy speech, there are 3 key issues that any policy speech *must* prove. This worksheet will help you develop each of those necessary arguments.

Issue 1: NEED

Prove that there is a need for change and create concern for the problem in your audience's minds.

A. What societal problem will your plan attempt to solve?

B. How significant is this problem?

C. Whom does it affect, and how?

D. How will you get your class audience to care about this problem?

Issue 2: PLAN

Outline a clear and practical solution to the problem.

Outline your preferred proposal for change in as much detail as you can foresee. **It is highly recommended that you do not come up with your own policy, but find a policy to advocate or adopt for a new context.** Remember to address such issues as how the plan will be administered, funded, implemented, and enforced.

Issue 3: PRACTICALITY

Prove that your plan will solve or significantly reduce the problem at hand, and that the advantages of this plan outweigh any potential disadvantages.

Provide specific reasons why your plan will work to solve the problem(s) established in Issue 1:

Make a list of the benefits that come from having your plan function the way in which it was designed:

Make a list of the alleged or actual disadvantages of your plan:

Give good reasons why the benefits of your plan outweigh the potential or real disadvantages:

Name potential counterarguments to your plan:

Instructor comments and suggestions:

Name _____

Topic _____

Unit 4

POLICY SPEECH

+ Excellent   **✓ Satisfactory**   **-- Needs improvement**   **0 Failed to complete**

INTRODUCTION   *Specific strengths and areas for improvement:*
Gained audience attention   _____
Established credibility   _____
Introduced topic clearly   _____
Related topic to audience   _____
Clear thesis/preview   _____

BODY: ORGANIZATION
Main points were clear   _____
Effective organizational pattern   _____
Effective connectives   _____

BODY: RESEARCH
Main points fully supported   _____
Adequate variety of sources   _____
Used credible sources   _____
Cited sources orally   _____

BODY: ARGUMENT
Sound and clear reasoning   _____
Clear problem (Need)   _____
Clear solution (Plan)   _____
Plan workable (Practicality)   _____
Advantages outweigh disadvantages _____
Addresses counterarguments   _____

BODY: AUDIENCE ADAPTATION
Adapted to audience   _____
Effective use of pathos   _____
Effective use of ethos   _____

CONCLUSION
Signaled end of speech   _____
Summarized main points   _____
Ended with artistic last line   _____

Q&A
Listened carefully to questions   _____
Managed session well   _____
Answered questions clearly
  and effectively   _____

CRITIQUE SHEET

DELIVERY

Maintained eye contact _____
Used vocal variety _____
Projected adequately _____
Pronunciation correct _____
Articulation clear _____
Rate appropriate _____
Paused effectively _____
Gestures purposeful _____
Proxemics effective _____
Mannerisms appropriate _____
Facial expression _____
Spoke fluently _____
Extemporaneous style _____
Effective use of speaking notes _____

VISUAL AIDS (optional)

Clear and easy to see _____
Professionally designed _____
Visual, rather than verbal _____
Incorporated into speech _____
Used technology appropriately _____
Added clarity to speech _____
Content _____

OUTLINE

Complete sentence format _____
Logical subordination _____
Labels included _____
Works Cited page _____
Accurate spelling _____
Correct grammar _____
Free of typos/errors _____

ADDITIONAL ITEMS

Topic challenging/appropriate _____
Completed in time limit _____
Fulfilled assignment requirements _____

Instructor comments and suggestions:

SafeAssign? Y / N

Time: _____

Score: _____ /250

Name _____

Topic _____

Unit 4

POLICY SPEECH

+ Excellent **✓ Satisfactory** **-- Needs improvement** **0 Failed to complete**

INTRODUCTION   *Specific strengths and areas for improvement:*
Gained audience attention   _____
Established credibility   _____
Introduced topic clearly   _____
Related topic to audience   _____
Clear thesis/preview   _____

BODY: ORGANIZATION
Main points were clear   _____
Effective organizational pattern _____
Effective connectives   _____

BODY: RESEARCH
Main points fully supported   _____
Adequate variety of sources   _____
Used credible sources   _____
Cited sources orally   _____

BODY: ARGUMENT
Sound and clear reasoning   _____
Clear problem (Need)   _____
Clear solution (Plan)   _____
Plan workable (Practicality)   _____
Advantages outweigh disadvantages _____
Addresses counterarguments   _____

BODY: AUDIENCE ADAPTATION
Adapted to audience   _____
Effective use of pathos   _____
Effective use of ethos   _____

CONCLUSION
Signaled end of speech   _____
Summarized main points   _____
Ended with artistic last line   _____

Q&A
Listened carefully to questions _____
Managed session well   _____
Answered questions clearly
  and effectively   _____

CRITIQUE SHEET

DELIVERY

Maintained eye contact _____

Used vocal variety _____

Projected adequately _____

Pronunciation correct _____

Articulation clear _____

Rate appropriate _____

Paused effectively _____

Gestures purposeful _____

Proxemics effective _____

Mannerisms appropriate _____

Facial expression _____

Spoke fluently _____

Extemporaneous style _____

Effective use of speaking notes _____

VISUAL AIDS (optional)

Clear and easy to see _____

Professionally designed _____

Visual, rather than verbal _____

Incorporated into speech _____

Used technology appropriately _____

Added clarity to speech _____

Content _____

OUTLINE

Complete sentence format _____

Logical subordination _____

Labels included _____

Works Cited page _____

Accurate spelling _____

Correct grammar _____

Free of typos/errors _____

ADDITIONAL ITEMS

Topic challenging/appropriate _____

Completed in time limit _____

Fulfilled assignment requirements _____

Instructor comments and suggestions:

SafeAssign? Y / N

Time: _____

Score: _____ /250

Listener _____

Speaker _____

Topic _____

Unit 4

POLICY SPEECH ORGANIZATION

Briefly outline the speaker's main points below. Then, reflect on how the speaker's organization affected her/his persuasive appeal.

Front page: Complete during the speech.

I. Introduction

    A. Attention-Getter:

    B. Credibility:

    C. Audience Adaptation:

    D. Thesis/Preview:

II. Body

III. Conclusion

    A. Review:

    B. "When to Clap" Line:

LISTENING SHEET

Back page: Complete after the speech is done.

What organizational pattern did the speaker use in this speech?

What aspects of the speaker's organization improved his/her persuasive appeal?

What aspects of the speaker's organization detracted from her/his persuasive appeal?

Listener _____

Speaker _____

Topic _____

Unit 4

POLICY SPEECH
RESEARCH

During the speech, record the speaker's source citations and types of supporting material. Then, reflect on the quality of the research as it related to development of the speaker's arguments.

Front page: Complete during the speech.

Sources:

Citation	**Type of Research**
Example	
Point 1:	
Dr. Jones (scientist)	Book
Association of Artificial Life Technology	Web site

LISTENING SHEET

Back page: Complete after the speech is done.

Did the speaker cite sources clearly throughout the speech?

Which main points were particularly well supported with research?

Which main points would have benefited from more support?

Which source(s) contributed most to the speaker's credibility? Why?

Which source citation(s) helped the speaker adapt to her/his class audience? Why?

What could the speaker have done differently with his/her sources to improve speaker credibility and audience adaptation?

Listener _____

Speaker _____

Topic _____

Unit 4

POLICY SPEECH
POLICY ISSUES

During the speech, record the speaker's claims and corresponding evidence for each of the three key policy issues. Then, rate the persuasive appeal/effectiveness of each argument on a scale of 1–5, with 1 being the least effective and 5 being the *most* effective.

Front page: Complete during the speech.

Need

Claim(s)   *Evidence*   *Effectiveness*

Plan

Claim(s)   *Evidence*   *Effectiveness*

Practicality

Claim(s)   *Evidence*   *Effectiveness*

LISTENING SHEET

Back page: Complete after the speech is done.

What counterarguments to this policy can you think of that the speaker either failed to address or failed to disprove sufficiently?

What suggestions can you provide this speaker for strengthening his/her audience appeal?

Listener _____

Speaker _____

Topic _____

Unit 4

POLICY SPEECH DELIVERY

Identify two of the speaker's delivery *strengths* (comment on any of the following: volume, pitch, rate, pauses, vocal variety, pronunciation, articulation, dialect, appearance, bodily action, gestures, and eye contact).

Identify two areas for *improvement* in the speaker's delivery (comment on any of the following: volume, pitch, rate, pauses, vocal variety, pronunciation, articulation, dialect, appearance, bodily action, gestures, and eye contact).

What speech preparation or practice techniques would you recommend to the speaker to improve her/his delivery?

LISTENING SHEET

UNIT 4 PERSUASIVE SPEAKING

Name _____

Topic _____

Unit 4

POLICY SPEECH

1. What do you feel were the major strengths of your speech? (Comment on arguments, persuasive language, audience adaptation, and coverage of key issues.)

2. What would you like to improve upon for your next speech?

3. What do you feel you improved from your last speech? (Comment on delivery, *ethos*, *pathos*, *logos*, evidence, audience adaptation, reasoning.)

SELF-EVALUATION SHEET

4. Give an example of how/where/when you might use a policy speech in your future.

5. How has your level of nervousness changed from your last speech?

UNIT 5

COMMEMORATIVE SPEAKING

Reading: *Invitation to Public Speaking*, Ch. 16 and review Ch. 10

Unit Objectives: Upon completion of this unit, you should understand:

- identify the different types of speeches delivered on special occasions

- understand the connection between commemoration and community values

- use language to make your speech appealing and memorable

- deliver a commemorative speech from manuscript

Assignment: Commemorative Speech

Prepare and present a 4–5 minute speech that pays tribute to a person, concept, organization, or institution. This speech will be delivered from manuscript. Organize your speech's main points according to those virtues exhibited by the subject you have chosen to amplify. Incorporate examples of both imagery and rhythm into your speech, and label them on your manuscript. **Be sure to select a topic that is praiseworthy for general audiences** (praising excessive alcohol/marijuana use or violence are bad topics for general audience, for instance). Making sure your topic is approved by your instructor will ensure you pick an appropriately praiseworthy topic. Prior to the delivery, submit a typed, double-spaced copy of your manuscript to your instructor. Upload that identical file (with your name removed) to SafeAssign. *Students who do not submit to SafeAssign may receive a zero on their speech.* Avoid spelling, typographical, or grammatical errors.

The Policy Speech Assignment Emphasizes the Following Skills:

- **Commemoration and Community Values:** Identify and illustrate the virtues possessed by your subject.

- **Argument:** Well-developed arguments should support your persuasive claims. Include clear logical appeals, appropriate emotional appeals, and thorough research.

- **Decorum:** Make speaking decisions that show appropriate attention to your audience, topic, and occasion.

- **Language Use:** Choose each word carefully and employ colorful, concrete, and evocative language.

- **Delivery:** Have a carefully polished delivery that employs dramatic pauses, vocal variations, and artistic phrasing. Because there is no research required for this speech, you are expected to put extra time into practicing your delivery.

by Carl R. Burgchardt, Ph.D.

The Commemorative Speech combines elements of informative and persuasive speaking; however, it is unlike previous assignments. It contains information about your subject, but it must go beyond simple biography to inspire your audience. In other words, the Commemorative Speech will be more than an encyclopedia entry that merely lists the historical facts of a person, concept, organization, thing, or institution. The purpose of the speech is to arouse and heighten admiration for your subject. You should try to penetrate to the essence of your topic, to generate a deep sense of appreciation and respect for the object of your praise. The assignment contains elements of persuasive speaking in that you are attempting to convince your audience that your subject is praiseworthy. Unlike deliberative speaking, however, the Commemorative Speech does not make explicit arguments, *per se*. Instead, the speech of tribute proceeds by amplifying the praiseworthy attributes of your subject. You must illustrate the positive virtues of your topic—things like honor, courage, compassion, faithfulness, and so forth.

In developing the virtues of your subject, it is important to show, *not simply tell*. In other words, you must use concrete, vivid language that illustrates and amplifies the virtues possessed by your subject. A person could simply assert, "My mother was unselfish." But the point is made much more vividly and convincingly by relaying an anecdote: "Many a night my mother never set a place for herself at the dinner table. She always told us kids that she had eaten at work. We never understood until much later that she went to bed hungry so that we had enough to eat." In the first instance, the speaker merely asserts a generalization; in the second example, the speaker illustrates in a dramatic fashion that the subject possesses a widely praised virtue.

Topic Selection

In selecting a topic for this assignment, be certain that the subject of your speech is indeed praiseworthy. In order for a human action to be considered praiseworthy, it must be **intentional** and **your audience must perceive it as virtuous**. For instance, a clumsy person might accidentally trip over a curb and inadvertently push a small child out of the path of a bus. While the effect of this action was to save the life of a child, the intent of the clumsy person was not courageous, so the behavior of the clumsy person is not really praiseworthy. In addition, a tragedy may happen to an individual that profoundly alters his or her life. For example, the subject of your speech may have developed cancer. Remember to praise the **virtuous reaction** to the tragedy and not the tragedy itself. In other words, don't praise a person for developing cancer; rather, praise the subject's heroic or dignified or wise reaction to the disease. **We praise intentional actions**, not accidents or misfortunes in themselves. Of course, if the subject of your speech is not human, then the question of intention is not really relevant.

Secondly, **be certain that your audience will consider the behavior or attribute of your subject to be praiseworthy**. No doubt, at the national convention of the Hell's Angels motorcycle gang, the ability to drink profusely might be considered a virtue. In that context, with that particular audience, a speaker might praise a fellow gang member for being a heavy drinker. But, in the general public, the ability to consume massive quantities of alcohol is not usually considered a virtue—quite the opposite. In another example, suppose a speaker wanted to praise rap music. Younger audiences may relish the driving beat and provocative lyrics of rap music, while older audiences may be offended by the social commentary and alienated by the lack of melody. Depending upon the composition of your audience, provocative lyrics may or may not be a praiseworthy attribute. In sum, then, before selecting a subject, be sure that your audience will share your sense of what is admirable. You must praise your subject in terms of the values your audience embraces.

In general, you should select a subject with which you are personally familiar and about which you care. There are two reasons for this. First, it is easier to invent appropriate materials for your subject if you already know all about it, and it will save you from having to do library research. Second, if you truly care about a subject, your personal conviction will shine through in the stylistic choices you make and in the quality of your delivery. If you are filled with genuine emotion, your speech will be enlivened by it.

Most students probably should select a person to praise. Parents, grandparents, siblings, spouses, "significant others," children, aunts and uncles, are natural and appropriate choices. You might also select a favorite teacher, coach, neighbor, minister, and the like. The more specific, familiar, and sincere your choice is, the better.

While it is more difficult, you also might choose objects or places like Rocky Mountain National Park, Old Town, the Trolley, the Poudre River, Moby Arena, the Oval, and so forth. These topics are more abstract, but it is still possible to praise them according to widely accepted virtues. You also could praise organizations, events, or institutions, such as United Way, the Boy Scouts, Colorado State University, the Fort Collins Symphony, the Bolder Boulder race, CSU Rams football games, and so on.

Abstract concepts are the most challenging topics, but it is theoretically possible to praise general ideas such as democracy, nature, freedom, meditation, art, music, or dance. However, students should be cautious about selecting such a subject: the more abstract the topic, the more difficult it is to invent and amplify virtues through the use of concrete language and specific stylistic devices. For the most part, we will assume that you will give a speech of tribute about people. Over the years, these have been the most consistently successful topics. *If you select another sort of topic, be certain to discuss this choice with your instructor well before your speech is due.*

Development and Organization

How does one invent and arrange materials for this speech? Unlike the informative and persuasive speeches, there are no sure-fire formats or structures for organizing the Commemorative Speech. However, there are some criteria or general principles that you may use to guide your efforts. First, it is a mistake to try to force your subject into a pre-established formula or to begin with preconceived ideas. On the other hand, it is an error to stare at a blank piece of paper or computer screen and hope for inspiration from above. The best way to invent appropriate materials for this speech is the stream-of-consciousness method. To do this, go to a quiet place where you can get into a contemplative mood. Then, meditate upon your subject. Immerse yourself in memories; read old letters; view photographs; fill yourself with warm, uplifting thoughts. When a positive memory occurs to you, write down the gist of it on an index card. At this point, don't be analytical or evaluative; just get it down on index cards. Concentrate on visual imagery, fragrances, bits of conversation, typical quotations, familiar activities, and the like. Allow the memories to pour out of you. The only discipline you must follow is to put each discrete impression or memory on a separate index card. This will make it easier to organize the speech later.

Some students are not comfortable giving a speech on a personal subject. In that case, it is perfectly fine to give a speech of tribute about a person or thing of national or international importance, from the past or present. Examples of appropriate subjects might be Martin Luther King, Mother Teresa, Albert Schweitzer, Susan B. Anthony, Wrigley Field, the Empire State Building, Niagara Falls, the Golden Gate Bridge, and so forth. Obviously, this sort of speech will require research, but the same inventional process that one uses for a personal topic still applies here. You must immerse yourself in the particulars of your subject's life or history. Surround yourself with biographies, autobiographies, diaries, letters and writings, photographs, audio and visual recordings, and other relevant materials. Allow these images, quotations, concepts, and feelings to fill up your mind and senses. Then, following the stream-of-consciousness method, write down discreet impressions on separate index cards in the same fashion as if you were doing a personal topic.

When you have accumulated a substantial stack of cards, try to sort them out into psychologically related themes or topics. Ask yourself, what does this bit of memory illustrate about my subject? For example, you might remember the smell of chocolate chip cookies baking in your mother's kitchen and associate this fragrance with a feeling of affection or devotion:

> Whenever I smell the delicious aroma of chocolate chip cookies baking in the oven, for a moment I become a small child again, sitting in my mother's kitchen. My mom knew how much I loved chocolate chip cookies. On special winter afternoons, just the two of us would make up a batch and feast on the gooey confections, hot from the oven. Love comes in many shapes and forms. For me, one kind of love smells like chocolate chip cookies, baking in the oven.

This quotation is merely one example of how you might translate a discreet memory into an illustration of a virtue. And, importantly, it is an illustration with which many in your audience will be able to relate. The use of concrete, descriptive language allows your audience to "experience" the memory and share your appreciation of it.

As you move through your stack of cards, sort the illustrations into separate themes or categories of virtues, such as love, intelligence, compassion, dignity, energy, sense of humor, integrity, and the like. As your categories emerge, you may do some shifting of cards to better illustrate and amplify the main themes of your speech. Some categories will be underdeveloped; others will be extensive. At this point, don't edit or be overly critical. Simply arrange the cards into piles and try to make each pile thematically unified. The only rule is, each stack of cards will illustrate, that is, **show**, not simply tell, a value or virtue that the audience is likely to accept.

Now, make a rough draft out of these stacks of index cards. Each pile will be converted into one or more paragraphs that illustrate a virtue. This is still early in the process, so don't worry about redundancy, choppiness, or stylistic quality. Just express your thoughts in sentences, taking care to expand upon every feeling and insight. When you are finished with this draft, you should have a series of paragraphs. Each paragraph should **illustrate** a virtue. Your rough draft can be compared to the stanzas of a prose poem. Each paragraph or "stanza" establishes and amplifies a distinctive virtue.

The next stage is to work on the internal development of each paragraph. Refine the progression of quotations, imagery, and description, so that one idea builds on another in a psychologically compelling way. Think about building suspense or a sense of mystery or wonder as each paragraph unfolds. Work on the unity and cohesiveness of individual paragraphs. Unity means that a paragraph is devoted to one theme. Cohesiveness means that all of the sentences in the paragraph "hold together" in an ordered, consistent way.

Take a pencil or marker and begin striking out redundancies and awkward sentences. Clarify ambiguities; work on internal transitions that link sentences; add material to complete ideas. At this point, begin to consciously refine or introduce metaphors, similes, and imagery. Enhance the natural rhythms of your prose by introducing or bolstering parallelism, repetition, and alliteration. These things may already be latent in your rough draft. Your job now is to bring them out and polish them. As you complete your revisions, you should be able to explain the position and function of each word, phrase, and sentence in the paragraph.

This is also the stage where you need to write an appropriate introduction and conclusion for your speech. Like any address, you must plan your introduction, body, and conclusion. In general, the introduction sets the mood, develops audience expectations, introduces the subject, and *subtly* announces the structure. You would *not* say: "Today I am going to argue that my mother is a wonderful person. I have three main arguments to support this claim: (1) she is compassionate; (2) she is brave; (3) she is imaginative." You *might* say something like:

> Compassion, courage, creativity—these three words are easy to say, but difficult to exemplify. They form a code, a plan of living that extraordinary people try to emulate. One such extraordinary person is my mother, Emily Ann Brown. If she had a motto, it would be "Compassion, courage, creativity."

Once you have completed the introduction, the body of the speech should be composed of three to six unified and cohesive paragraphs that establish and amplify the virtues of your subject. The conclusion restates and synthesizes the values of the speech. It also provides a *truly* memorable ending line, often returning to a concept or quotation used in the introduction. In the hypothetical example we have been using, the speech might well end with the words, "Compassion, courage, creativity."

No one structure or plan is ideal for the Commemorative Speech. Select an organizational scheme that matches you and your subject. Don't be afraid to use the devices of drama and suspense. For example, in one memorable speech, a student began her speech with a vivid description of a funeral. The speaker figuratively brought this scene before the eyes of the audience. She explained that hundreds of people were gathered for the funeral of a high school principal. During the course of the funeral, the speaker described her thoughts and memories of this outstanding educator. At the very end of the speech, the student revealed that the high school principal was her father. This revelation, which came as a total surprise to the audience, brought all of the speaker's remarks into startling focus and resulted in a poignant moment. The use of a surprising revelation at the end of a speech can be highly effective, but don't abuse this technique. Another student told a tale of how he lost his "best friend." After waxing nostalgic about all of the wonderful adventures he shared with his friend, he related the fateful day when his playmate fell from the top of the jungle gym and was killed instantly. In the last line of the speech, the speaker revealed that his best friend was a hamster! Although the loss of a pet is a sad thing, this student cynically manipulated the audience, and the reaction of his classmates was dismay and anger.

As the above examples indicate, time and place do not have to be treated in a strictly chronological way; indeed, the Commemorative Speech is often stronger if it does not follow a conventional, informative pattern. A better course is to select a structure that allows you to focus on virtues rather than a dull narrative that recounts "this happened, then that happened, then this happened." A speech may begin with the end of a person's life or entail flashbacks; it may begin with a characteristic saying, pose, place, or feeling. It may end in the same ways. The goal is to *show* to the audience the virtues of your subject, not to convey abstract or mundane details about birth, childhood, education, career, retirement, etc.

Delivery

Unlike the other speeches of the semester, this assignment will be read from manuscript. That means you will deliver the speech exactly as it is written. Since this is a manuscript speech, there is no excuse for falling outside of the time limits. Therefore, when you have finished polishing and editing your speech, you will need to time it exactly. Cut or expand the speech to fit precisely between 4 and 5 minutes. Then, produce a clean manuscript to hand in to your instructor. This should be double-spaced and be free of typos, and spelling, grammar, and punctuation errors. Remember to hand in two copies of your speech, as you have done with previous assignments. A substantial part of your grade will be based on the quality of the manuscript you submit.

Once you have accomplished these tasks, prepare a reading copy of your manuscript—the one you will use to deliver the speech. The reading copy should be marked up with underlining and instructions on pauses, intonations, volume, and so forth. The reading copy may be typed triple-spaced or printed in oversized type. That is up to you. Many students find it helpful to glue their sheets of paper to stiff cardboard for ease of handling, or to encase the manuscript in "slick sheets"—hole-punched, plastic sheaths that can be inserted into a notebook. In any event, prepare your manuscript in a way that will allow you maximum ease and freedom when delivering your speech. You should be able to hold your manuscript with one hand, leaving the other hand free for page turning or gesturing.

To be successful, you must practice reading your speech aloud on many occasions. You should rehearse the speech until it is nearly memorized (or actually memorized). Above all, on the day of the speech, you must avoid the impression that you are reading your manuscript for the first time. You should be so familiar with your manuscript, that once you begin a sentence or a line of text, you can finish it without looking at it. As you are delivering your speech, try to maintain good eye contact with the audience. You want to **sound** spontaneous and sincere, even though every word has been carefully planned and rehearsed. Reliance on the manuscript is analogous to the way a train keeps on the tracks. The train has great momentum, and will keep moving whether it is on the tracks or not. The tracks simply guide the force of the train. So too, the lines of the manuscript are the "tracks" that keep your speech moving forward in a precise direction. Finally, think of this speech as a performance. Delivery of the Commemorative Speech is more akin to acting than to ordinary speech delivery. You should use dramatic pauses, vary the tone of your voice, vary the volume and rate, and use gestures and facial expressions to underscore the meaning of the words.

The best way to approach this assignment is to give a sincere speech from your heart. If you conscientiously attempt to use the stylistic devices discussed in your textbook, and if you practice, the chances are good that you will surprise yourself and your classmates, and you will deliver the most eloquent speech of your life. Moreover, students in the past have used this assignment as an opportunity to express exactly how they feel about special people in their lives. Parents, spouses, relatives, children, grandparents, coaches, special teachers, and friends would all be deeply moved if they received a copy of your manuscript as a gift. Or, if the subject of your speech is deceased, this is an excellent opportunity to create a lasting tribute that friends and relatives would cherish. Sometimes, these speeches are actually given outside of class. One student was expected to make a speech at her parents' twenty-fifth wedding anniversary, and she used this assignment to develop the oration. Her family was truly moved by the smoothness of her delivery and the eloquence of her language.

Sometimes students feel that they don't know anyone famous or heroic or successful enough to praise publicly in a speech. They are embarrassed that their subject is not wealthy or powerful. But, as we all know, seemingly ordinary individuals often lead extraordinary lives, but they do it quietly and privately. Hard work, dignity, integrity, and love of life are wonderful virtues that are exhibited every day by people who may not be "successful" by materialistic standards. The following model speech is an example of how you might go about praising so-called "ordinary" people.

Sample Commemorative Speech Manuscript
for Analysis and Discussion

Note on labeling stylistic devices: In this manuscript, stylistic devices and some stage prompts are included in parentheses. Your instructor may prefer that you underline or highlight stylistic devices and write in labels by hand. Use whatever method your instructor advises and allows for accuracy and clarity.

SPCM 200, [Section]
[Date]

Lina

by Katherine Gould

(Paragraph develops an extended tree metaphor and employs parallelism) Like a quivering Aspen (simile) she stood; with her roots firmly planted in the soil of wisdom (metaphor), with her trunk steadfast and strong against the ferocious winds of time (metaphor), with her branches offered to the world that sought to cut her down an embrace of compassion (metaphor), and with her leaves spread toward the sun in reverence for the giver of life. She stood. I speak to you not of a famous woman, but of a woman who was a friend, a minister, a mother—my mother, Lina (antithesis). She was a friend whose wisdom aided those in need, a minister whose strength kept her going against enormous odds, and a mother whose compassion and reverence influenced her child to look at life and the people in it as caring and beautiful (parallelism).

While I know I shall always remember moments with my mother, like the times when we read the *Little House on the Prairie* collection and Greek mythology as bedtime stories, or the times she played soccer with me to help me practice for a big game, I know I will remember her mostly for the conversations we had. She was wise. During these times she passed on knowledge about her life, mistakes she made, and the wisdom she had learned along the way. She talked to me as an equal. She talked to me as someone who had a valid viewpoint always worth hearing and considering, and she talked to me in order to push me to make me think harder (repetition "she talked"). She was always bringing up topics that others might have thought to be too difficult. She spoke of politics, sex, depression, and yes—even death. She pushed me to learn more and ask questions. There is one such conversation that stands out more than any other. A conversation that showed her wisdom.

Picture a young single mother sitting at the kitchen table with a bowl full of cherries and her five-year old daughter. Try to imagine the wisdom and strength it took for this woman to tell her daughter that she had breast cancer, that she was sick, that she could die (parallelism), and that she might not be around in the near future. My mother was wise. She told me what to expect: from hospital trips and doctor visits, to the possible best and worst of the situation, to the expected and the unknown. She helped me to understand so that I wouldn't be afraid of what lay ahead. The rest of that year and continuing on into the next was hard, but my mother remained strong.

Through the years that followed my mother's battle with cancer only became fiercer. After her first experience with cancer we crossed our fingers and waited to see if she was out of the clear. One month, two months, six months, a year (parallelism), time passed and cancer's memory was fading fast until my mother went for a checkup and once again a lump was found. But unlike the first time, when the doctors had been able to remove all the cancer through surgery and chemotherapy, this time they took her breast as well. It was part of what defined her as a woman, and it took all her strength to remain standing strong and appear whole. She had other responsibilities to think about—fulfilling her role as a minister and counselor, friend and confidant, mother and teacher (parallelism). It took tremendous strength to deal with this. She did not dwell, did not crumble under pressure. She stood. Strong and tall, ready to move onto the challenges that were yet to come.

Time passed again. This time we hoped but were less naïve. This time cancer's memory did not fade. This time we had to face the ordeals that my mother would endure. She took what she had learned and the strength she had gained and opened her arms and heart to the world. Through these trials and tribulations she grew more compassionate and more reverent. Before her bouts with cancer, my mother gave sermons every Sunday, headed committees and made visits, but after the second battle with cancer she undertook a more important role. She became the rock that people leaned on (metaphor). I remember evenings where we would receive a call from someone in need of a shoulder to cry on and she would spend the next three hours talking to them. My mother's door was open to anyone; even people outside her parish would visit because they had heard she could help.

As wise, strong, and compassionate as she was, her time was coming to an end. During the summer before I was to start my sixth grade year, she once again was diagnosed with cancer; however, this time it had spread to her bones. Her x-rays were pictures of dark, demented, disturbing (alliteration) shadows that were haunting (metaphor) my mother's body. The only hope lay in a bone marrow transplant, but her life was not meant to continue. During the transplant process, my mother contracted pneumonia and was placed on a respirator. This action later lead to complications and on May 3, 1994 she died. Her tree no longer stands, her roots are no longer there, her trunk no longer withstands the winds of time, her branches no longer embrace the world and her leaves have fallen. She was my mother, Lina (concluding lines return to the extended metaphor, employing imagery and mirroring the introduction. They also use parallel structure).

Sample Commemorative Speech Manuscript
for Analysis and Discussion

Note on labeling stylistic devices: In this manuscript, stylistic devices and some stage prompts are included in parentheses. Your instructor may prefer that you underline or highlight stylistic devices and write in labels by hand. Use whatever method your instructor advises and allows for accuracy and clarity.

SPCM 200, [Section]
[Date]

The Matthews House

by Tatum Cochran

When children transition from being in foster care or a juvenile justice facility to being adults in society, the system often forgets about them (personification). These young adults frequently have not had stable adult influences, and do not know many of the skills necessary for a positive transition into adulthood. The Matthews House is an organization that is committed to providing resources and support for these youth that empower them to take control of their lives. The mission, staff, programs, and relationship building opportunities that the Matthews House has all embody the committed nature of the organization. This local nonprofit has been important to me because the people there have helped me become closer to the Fort Collins community, and I hope through this speech you are all able to see the commitment this organization has to making our community a better place.

The Matthews House's mission is committed to providing resources that help young adults develop several important skills necessary to move into a stable, independent living situation. The organization assists the youth by helping find safe and affordable housing, helping find physical and mental health resources, helping find employment, helping find education, and helping find programs that encourage independent living and social skills (parallelism). These resources and skills act as building blocks for the youth, with which they can create an independent life (simile).

Staff members and volunteers at the Matthews House are gladiators, fighting for the rights of the youth who are part of the program (metaphor). These dedicated adults provide a stable example for the participants, and are committed to establishing a supportive community where these transitioning youth can thrive. The principle "Tell me and I will forget. Show me and I may remember. Involve me and I will understand" holds true for all of the staff and volunteers in the organization. In order to volunteer with the Matthews House, one must undergo a background check and a training session, to ensure that the youth are getting support from trustworthy and well-prepared adults. There are a variety of ways community members can get involved with the organization, from planning fundraisers to cooking dinner once a week at the house. The commitment to the youth in the program, and to the Fort Collins community at large, that these adults show is truly remarkable.

The activities and programs offered by the Matthews House are not only fun; they are useful (antithesis). These opportunities, such as GED classes, rock climbing groups, and cooking classes provide skills for the youth involved, as well as giving a chance to improve social skills in a structured environment. The programs are committed to giving the young people an enjoyable way to learn important skills necessary for independent living. There are physical activities, educational support groups, recreation programs, and family wellness opportunities available, as well as other fun and instructive ways to get involved.

The Matthews House also provides a mentorship program, where they match one adult with one youth participant for a period of 6 months up to several years. This relationship develops a sense of stability for the young person, and gives the mentor an opportunity to better understand the experiences of many young people in Fort Collins. Mentors and mentees can do any number of things together, from getting coffee to writing resumes, from playing baseball to cooking dinner (parallelism). In order to match up youth and adults, the staff at the Matthews House hold interviews for both participants and potential mentors. This process helps ensure that the relationship will be beneficial for both parties. By creating a caring, compassionate, and considerate environment, this relationship-building aspect of the organization is important for transitioning youth (alliteration). In order to show the young participants the possibilities their futures may hold, several mentors are previous participants in the program.

The Matthews House is committed to providing a stable and safe, happy and healthy environment for the young adults who are in the transition process between the foster care or the juvenile justice system and life as adults in society (alliteration). This organization makes Fort Collins a closer and more supportive community, and I hope that all of you find a cause, like this one, that makes you optimistic for our community's future.

UNIT 5   COMMEMORATIVE SPEAKING

Name_____

Date_____

Unit 5

COMMEMORATIVE SPEECH

Propose two potential topics for your Commemorative Speech. List them below, in order of preference, and explain why you think your subjects are praiseworthy.

Topic 1:

List 2–3 virtues exemplified by your subject, and briefly note the anecdotes or examples you will use to illustrate each virtue.

Topic 2:

List 2–3 virtues exemplified by your subject, and briefly note the anecdotes or examples you will use to illustrate each virtue.

Instructor Comments:

Topic 1 __ Approved __ Not Approved

Topic 2 __ Approved __ Not Approved

Name _____

Topic _____

Unit 5

COMMEMORATIVE SPEECH

+ Excellent   ✓ **Satisfactory**   **-- Needs improvement**   **0 Failed to complete**

INTRODUCTION   *Specific strengths and areas for improvement:*

Gained audience attention   _____

Set proper mood   _____

Clear/artistic preview   _____

BODY

Main points were clear   _____

Virtues clearly identified   _____

Virtues well illustrated   _____

Concrete language/vivid
   descriptions   _____

Use of imagery   _____

Use of rhythm   _____

Pathos   _____

CONCLUSION

Reinforced mood   _____

Virtues restated   _____

Meaningful/artistic last line   _____

DELIVERY

Maintained eye contact   _____

Used vocal variety   _____

Projected adequately   _____

Pronunciation correct   _____

Articulation clear   _____

Rate appropriate   _____

Paused effectively   _____

Gestures purposeful   _____

Proxemics effective   _____

Mannerisms appropriate   _____

Facial expression   _____

Spoke fluently   _____

Effective use of manuscript   _____

CRITIQUE SHEET

MANUSCRIPT
Labeled stylistic devices   _____

Accurate spelling   _____

Correct grammar   _____

Corresponds to presentation   _____

Free of typos/errors   _____

ADDITIONAL ITEMS
Subject praiseworthy   _____

Completed in time limit   _____

Fulfilled assignment
   requirements   _____

Instructor comments and suggestions:

SafeAssign? Y / N

Time: _____

Score: _____ **/100**

Name _____

Topic _____

Unit 5

COMMEMORATIVE SPEECH

+ Excellent   **✓ Satisfactory**   **-- Needs improvement**   **0 Failed to complete**

INTRODUCTION   ***Specific strengths and areas for improvement:***
Gained audience attention   _____
Set proper mood   _____
Clear/artistic preview   _____

BODY
Main points were clear   _____
Virtues clearly identified   _____
Virtues well illustrated   _____
Concrete language/vivid
   descriptions   _____
Use of imagery   _____
Use of rhythm   _____
Pathos   _____

CONCLUSION
Reinforced mood   _____
Virtues restated   _____
Meaningful/artistic last line   _____

DELIVERY
Maintained eye contact   _____
Used vocal variety   _____
Projected adequately   _____
Pronunciation correct   _____
Articulation clear   _____
Rate appropriate   _____
Paused effectively   _____
Gestures purposeful   _____
Proxemics effective   _____
Mannerisms appropriate   _____
Facial expression   _____
Spoke fluently   _____
Effective use of manuscript   _____

CRITIQUE SHEET

MANUSCRIPT

Labeled stylistic devices   _____
Accurate spelling   _____
Correct grammar   _____
Corresponds to presentation   _____
Free of typos/errors   _____

ADDITIONAL ITEMS

Subject praiseworthy   _____
Completed in time limit   _____
Fulfilled assignment
   requirements   _____

Instructor comments and suggestions:

SafeAssign? Y / N

Time: _____

Score: _____ **/100**

Speaker _____

Topic _____

Unit 5

COMMEMORATIVE SPEECH COMMEMORATION AND COMMUNITY VALUES

Identify the virtues the speaker chose to illustrate, and the examples/descriptions used to amplify them. Then, reflect upon how well the speaker tapped into community values in this speech.

Front page: Complete during the speech.

Virtue   **Example**

Back page: Complete after the speech is done.

Was the speaker's choice of virtues well-adapted to the class audience and the assignment? Why or why not?

What suggestions can you give to the speaker for improving the amplification of virtues in this speech?

What have you learned from the commemorative speaking round about the relationship between emotional appeal in speeches and community values?

Listener _____

Speaker _____

Topic _____

Unit 5

COMMEMORATIVE SPEECH STYLE AND LANGUAGE

Identify examples of imagery and rhythm in the speech. Then, reflect on how the speaker's language choices enhanced or detracted from the speech.

Front page: Complete during the speech.

As you hear them in the speech, write down examples of the following stylistic devices:

Concrete words:

Metaphor:

Simile:

Personification:

Alliteration:

Parallelism:

Repetition:

Antithesis:

Back page: Complete after the speech is done.

What imagery device was most effective in this speech, and why?

How could the speaker have used imagery and/or rhythm differently to improve his/her speech?

Comment on the speaker's delivery. Did the speaker use vocal variety, pauses, eye contact, etc., to maximize the effectiveness of her/his language choices?

Listener _____   123

Speaker _____

Topic _____

Unit 5

COMMEMORATIVE SPEECH DELIVERY

Identify two of the speaker's delivery *strengths* (comment on volume, pitch, rate, pauses, vocal variety, pronunciation, articulation, dialect, appearance, bodily action, gestures, and eye contact).

Identify two areas for *improvement* in the speaker's delivery (comment on volume, pitch, rate, pauses, vocal variety, pronunciation, articulation, dialect, appearance, bodily action, gestures, and eye contact).

What speech preparation or practice techniques would you recommend to the speaker to improve her/his delivery?

UNIT 5 COMMEMORATIVE SPEAKING

Name _____

Topic _____

Unit 5

COMMEMORATIVE SPEECH

1. What do you feel were the major strengths of your speech? (Comment on organization, delivery, and use of linguistic devices.)

2. How have your speech composition and delivery skills improved over the course of the semester?

3. Give an example of how/where/when you might use this type of speech in your future.

4. What information or skills will you take away from this speech for use in future personal or professional contexts?

5. How has your nervousness improved throughout the semester?